I0555349

FINAL AFFAIR
ARRANGEMENTS

FINAL AFFAIR
ARRANGEMENTS
Informational Guide and Workbook

ELAINE LOZINSKI, CEA

BIG MOOSE
PUBLISHING

©2023 Elaine Lozinski, CEA

Published by: Big Moose Publishing
PO Box 127 Site 601 RR#6 Saskatoon, SK CANADA S7K 3J9
www.bigmoosepublishing.com

All rights reserved. No part of this book may be used or reproduced by any means, graphic, electronic, or mechanical, including photocopying, recording, taping or by any information storage retrieval system without the written permission of the author.

Because of the dynamic nature of the Internet, any web addresses or links contained in this book may have changed since publication and may no longer be valid. The views expressed in this work are solely those of the author and do not necessarily reflect the views of the publisher, and the publisher hereby disclaims any responsibility for them.

This book and its worksheets are of Canadian origin and therefore use language, terminology, and legal requirements as it pertains to Canadian citizens. If the reader lives outside of Canada, please contact proper authorities and professionals to confirm your region's laws and government specifications.

The intent of the author is to offer information of a general nature to assist with final affair planning and preparation and is not intended to replace the advice of professionals. In the event information in this book is used, the author and the publisher assume no responsibility for actions taken. Readers should use their own judgment and/or consult professional and legal experts for specific applications to their individual situations.

Although the author has extensively fact checked to ensure accuracy and completeness of the information contained in this book, the author assumes no responsibility for errors, inaccuracies, omissions or inconsistencies herein.

Cover photo supplied by Dean Mitchell, Getty Images. Stock photo used for illustrative purposes only. Any persons depicted in content are models only.

ISBN: 978-1-989840-43-6

Big Moose Publishing 01/2023

For Harold and his beloved Betty,
where this journey all began.

DISCLAIMER

The information presented within *Just in Case: Final Affair Arrangements* is meant for guidance only while preparing your final affairs. It is not intended to replace the advice of professionals.

Just in Case recognizes the importance of professional advice in the various fields involved with final affair and estate planning. Therefore, we strongly suggest you seek out the advice of a professional while preparing your final affair documents, to answer the specific questions unique to your situation, and to provide you with the best possible advice.

For questions surrounding death benefits, legal documents, funeral costs, philanthropy and the charitable sector, tax laws, estate requirements and laws, or for any other areas or questions, please consult the following professionals:

Estate Lawyer	Accountant
Financial Planner	Banker
Realtor	Insurance Agent
Funeral Director	Charitable Representative
Doctor	Government Agent
Personal Planning Advisor	Final Affair Consultant

No portion of this publication may be reproduced in any manner without the written permission of the author.

Contents

INTRODUCTION i

JUST IN CASE FINAL AFFAIR ARRANGEMENTS iii

PART 1 FINAL AFFAIR ARRANGEMENTS 1
FINAL AFFAIRS: WHAT DOES THIS MEAN? 3
PRE-PLANNING: WHY IS IT IMPORTANT? 5
FAMILY DISCUSSION 9
INFORMATION LOCATION AND UPKEEP 13
HOW TO START (AND FINISH) PLANNING YOUR AFFAIRS 15

PART 2 FINAL AFFAIR CATEGORIES 17
Section 1 PERSONAL INFORMATION 19
Section 2 CONTACT LISTS 23
Section 3 FINANCIAL INFORMATION 25
Section 4 POWER OF ATTORNEY 29
Section 5 HEALTH CARE DIRECTIVE 37
Section 6 WILL AND ESTATE INFORMATION 43
    6.1 Terminology 45
    6.2 Choosing an Executor 47
    6.3 Creating a Will 54
    6.4 Checklists for Survivors and Executors 64
    6.5 Estate Administration 69
Section 7 FUNERAL/MEMORIAL ARRANGEMENTS 79
Section 8 IMPORTANT DOCUMENTATION 87
Section 9 FAMILY INFORMATION 89
Section 10 PHILANTHROPY AND CHARITY 93
Section 11 OTHER CONSIDERATIONS 97
    11.1 Pet Care 97
    11.2 Housing 98
    11.3 Retirement Plan 100
    11.4 De-clutter 101
    11.5 Shared Learning 102
IN CLOSING 103

PART 3 WORKSHEETS 105

PERSONAL INFORMATION 107
1.1 Personal Information 109
1.2 Medical Information 111
1.3 Employment Information 115
1.4 Technology 117
1.4-1 Technology: Online Services 119
1.5 Military Service Information 121
1.6 Legal Information 123
1.7 Personal Information: Other... 125

CONTACT LISTS 127
2.1 Personal Contacts: In case of Emergency, Death, or First to Know................................ 129
2.2 Contacts: Other 131

FINANCIAL INFORMATION.. 133
3.1-1 Financial Institutions 135
3.1-2 Auto Charges or Deposits... 137
3.1-3 Debit and Credit Cards 139
3.1-4 Safety Deposit Box 141
3.2-1 Income 143
3.2-2 Investments/Trusts.. 145
3.3-3 Tax Returns 147
3.3-1 Mortgage.. 149
3.3-2 Loans 151
3.3-3 Support.. 153
3.3-4 Lease Agreements 155
3.3-5 Liabilities: Other 157
3.4-1 Power and Energy 159
3.4-2 Phone Services 161
3.4-3 Water and Municipal/City Tax 163
3.4-4 Internet and TV Streaming Services 165
3.4-5 Utilities: Other.. 167
3.5-1 Home... 169
3.5-2 Farm Land... 171
3.5-3 Business 173
3.5-4 Vacation Property... 175
3.5-5 Real Estate 177
3.5-6 Vehicle(s).. 179

3.5-7 Recreational Vehicle(s) 181

3.5-8 Major Assets: Other 183

3.5-9 Major Assets: Notes 185

3.6-1 Life Insurance 187

3.6-2 Accidental Insurance 189

3.6-3 Disability Insurance 191

3.6-4 Medical Insurance 193

3.6-5 Home Insurance 195

3.6-6 Vacation Home Insurance 197

3.6-7 Farm/Crop Insurance 199

3.6-8 Vehicle Insurance 201

3.6-9 Recreational Vehicle(s) Insurance 203

3.6-10 Insurance: Other 205

3.6-11 Notes 207

POWER OF ATTORNEY 209

4.1 Power of Attorney 211

HEALTH CARE DIRECTIVE 213

5.1 Health Care Directive 215

5.1-1 Health Care Directive: Notes 216

WILL AND ESTATE INFORMATION 217

6.1 Will and Estate Information 219

6.2 Will and Estate: Notes 221

6.3 Letter of Intent 223

FUNERAL/MEMORIAL ARRANGEMENTS 225

7.1 Funeral Home Information 227

7.2 Funeral/Memorial Service 229

7.3 Interment 231

7.4 Obituary/Eulogy 233

7.5 Funeral/Memorial: Notes 235

IMPORTANT DOCUMENTATION 237

8.1 Important Documentation 239

FAMILY INFORMATION 241

9.1-1 Family History: You 243

9.1-2 Parents 245

9.1-3 Siblings 247

9.1-4 Grandparents 251

9.1-5 Children 255

9.1-6 Grandchildren 259

9.1-7 Nieces & Nephews 263

9.1-8 Uncles & Aunts 267

9.1-9 Family: Other 273

9.2-1 Important Dates 275

9.2-2 Address History 277

9.2-3 Family Memories/Stories 279

9.2-4 Family Data: Other 281

9.3-1 Letters to Loved Ones 283

9.3-2 Memorabilia 285

9.3-3 Family: Other Information 287

PHILANTHROPY AND CHARITY 289

10.1 Philanthropy/Charity 291

OTHER CONSIDERATIONS 293

11.1 Pets 295

11.2 Housing 297

11.3 Retirement Plan 299

11.4 De-Clutter 303

11.5 Shared Knowledge 305

11.6 Final Thoughts 307

About the Author 309

Acknowledgments 311

Request a *Just in Case: Final Affair Arrangements* Seminar 313

INTRODUCTION

J ust in Case was born out of love. A husband was instructed by his doctors to get his affairs in order due to a medical condition. He wanted to ensure his wife knew and understood all necessary and important information for when he wouldn't be around. Together they gathered their wills, the family's finances, and other essential matters into a binder. It was all in one place and easy to find.

When the time came to use this information, the family found the advanced preparation allowed them to spend quality time together, sharing memories rather than being burdened with searching for documents. The family also found they did not encounter stress from countless phone calls and hurried decisions, and there was no need to second-guess their loved one's intentions because it had already been written down.

The concept of a universal plan to help others organize their affairs in an unexpected death took root, and *Just in Case* was created.

For incapacity, end of life, or other support needs.
For those who are required to act on your behalf.

Just in Case.

JUST IN CASE
FINAL AFFAIR ARRANGEMENTS

A s you consider getting your affairs in order, the goal of *Just in Case* is to empower you to make your own decisions before something happens; decisions that you may not be able to communicate otherwise.

BENEFITS OF JUST IN CASE

Just in Case provides suggestions for things you may not consider on your own. This book allows you to educate yourself and to become familiar with various processes and terminology. It also gives you the opportunity to write down your questions. You can prepare for professional appointments by having completed documentation prior to the meeting, hopefully saving you both time and money. Most importantly, it will give you peace of mind and ease any burden for your loved ones in difficult times.

Works in Three Ways:

1. EDUCATION

Just in Case provides detailed information and explanations on over ten different final affair areas. It describes and identifies the importance of each area while providing definitions and examples, elevating your confidence, and expanding your knowledge for each subject.

2. GUIDANCE

Just in Case walks you through the process of each final affair section, suggesting things to consider and include while planning. It provides fill-in-the-blank work sheets for organization and allows you space to add other information that you may see fit.

***Just in Case* is a guide <u>only</u> and not meant to replace the work of professionals.**

3. INFORMATION STORAGE

Just in Case offers an approach to gather all your final affair information and documents in one place or, at the very least, to indicate where the information can be found. Remember, your information is no good unless someone can find it.

Who should use Just in Case?

***Just in Case* is for you**. Use this book to find out what it means to get your affairs in order, ensure your intentions and preferences are well thought out and documented, and review or update your existing plans.

***Just in Case* is for your role as Power of Attorney or Executor.** This valuable resource tool outlines the responsibilities of these roles, provides you with information and will confirm the documentation you will require to fulfil these duties.

***Just in Case* is for your loved ones**. It is a perfect guide to assist your parents or other loved ones as they plan their affairs. It is an excellent agent to foster discussion about final affair planning and to confirm their information, documentation, and wishes.

Be proud of becoming proactive in your final affair planning! Remember, the hard work you do with *Just in Case* will give you peace of mind and will be invaluable to others when the time comes. Even the smallest amount of work completed is extremely helpful to those who must look after your affairs.

Every large journey begins with one small step.

Thank you for commitment.

***Just in Case*.**

PART 1

FINAL AFFAIR
ARRANGEMENTS

FINAL AFFAIRS:
WHAT DOES THIS MEAN?

Final affair planning is sometimes referred to as getting your affairs in order, estate planning or succession planning. But what does that really mean?

Simply put, it means to organize the things relating to your personal life and gather them together for your surviving partner, family, Power of Attorney or Executor. While it is often associated with dying and end of life, planning your affairs is helpful for emergencies, incapacity and other support needs or situations, including temporary assistance or if Power of Attorney comes into effect.

Final affair planning is more involved than most people expect! It goes beyond identifying your financial information or creating a Will. *Just in Case* has identified several different areas to consider when preparing your final affairs, all with the purpose of providing information to those who will require it.

PRE-PLANNING:
WHY IS IT IMPORTANT?

You matter. Your life is important.

Pre-planning allows you to make plans for you and your family, your life and your health. It empowers you to make your own decisions before something happens, decisions that you may not be able to communicate otherwise.

BAD EXPERIENCES

We all have heard stories or have personally experienced bad circumstances after a passing. Often, when final affair information and documentation are required, the situation is chaotic. Emotions run high and often family members scramble to find what is necessary, or are called on to make tough decisions while under strain. For loved ones who must manage affairs, pre-planning helps reduce the uncertainty, stress, and confusion due to a lack of clear direction, while hopefully reducing the chances of family disputes.

YOUR RESPONSIBILITY

Throughout life you plan for education, weddings, vacations, and retirement; plan for this too. Death is a part of life; take the time to address it. Don't leave this big job for someone else. Being prepared is not only necessary, but it is your responsibility. The final affair areas of *Just in Case* must be addressed by someone eventually. If you don't plan in advance, decisions will be left to others who may not know or understand your intentions.

YOU KNOW YOUR STUFF

How many of us have a "unique" filing system? For example, are your tax returns in a shoebox under your bed? Would somebody know where your financial information is kept? Perhaps you have a storage unit across town where you keep an old car that you had purchased twenty-five years ago. Does someone know where all of your assets are and how to access them? Have you always wanted a funeral at the lake with your ashes scattered over the bow of a boat? Does your spouse or family know what you want by way of funeral or memorial plans?

You know what your wishes are. You know the location of your papers. You know your assets, liabilities, and all other information that will be required. Why leave it for someone else to guess? Be responsible and assist your loved ones before the time comes, and you are not able to help.

GET EDUCATED

Do you know that a Power of Attorney can spend your money however he or she sees fit? Planning final affairs involves some of the most important and potentially dangerous legal documents out there. Pre-planning allows time for education. Take the time to educate yourself on each final affair area, particularly the legal sections. Become familiar with the processes and language, outline your questions, ensure you know how the documents work and understand what you are signing.

PRE-PLANNING PROCRASTINATION

We don't want to think about our own death or incapacitation, especially while we are healthy. We think it's something that isn't going to happen to us...at least not for many years; it's far into our future – right? It is entirely natural to be reluctant to think about an emergency or end of life situation. It is also much easier to procrastinate the task. Perhaps one or two of the following excuses may feel familiar to you:

"It's a lot of work."
"It's too time consuming."
"There is too much to think about."
"It's too overwhelming and intimidating."

We are not going to lie. Yes, it is a lot of work. There is much to consider and decide, and there is a great deal of information to trace and record. It is important to understand that it would take someone else double the time it takes you to do this work, and even more time if information is not gathered or known. Go slow and break the job into smaller pieces. This approach will not make the task so large and daunting.

"My spouse took/takes care of these things. I assume everything is fine."

Sometimes there is one person in a relationship who generally takes care of the household finances. While this works great for some couples, it is still important that both people understand how things work and why.

If your partner has passed on or if your spouse is still alive, but has always taken care of the financial matters, it may be time to become more familiar with this aspect of your life. Take the time to educate yourself, learn more about your own final affair areas, and update your information.

"I have physical disabilities (cataracts, hearing issues, arthritis, Parkinson's, ALS, etc.) that prevent me from completing these tasks."

Sometimes disabilities may be limiting, but it does not make the task impossible. It is never too late to start! Enlist the help of a trusted friend or family member, or perhaps you can invite your Power of Attorney or Executor to assist you. They can be your eyes, ears, and hands to help you work through the job.

"It can wait."
"Nothing is going to happen to me for years!"
"I don't want to think about my own death!"

Let's face it, death and illness are a part of life. Sudden events such as accidents, heart attacks, or strokes, to name a few, can cause unexpected death or incapacitation at any time, or at any age.

This may sound a bit cliché, but pre-planning affairs really does give you peace of mind. While we will never know what the future holds for us, we can at least know that we have helped our loved ones in the best way possible, just in case something were to happen to us.

"I don't want to deal with this stuff. Let my family take care of it when I'm gone!"

Many people assume that when they are unable, their families can take care of matters; however, this is not the case. In fact, when there are no pre-arrangements made, the government and the courts have a predetermined way of administrating affairs, especially by way of Health Care Directive, Power of Attorney, and your estate.

Learn about what happens if your affairs are not taken care of. Decide now how you want your affairs carried out. Besides, does anyone really want the court system interfering with your personal matters?

People have many reasons to delay their planning. Given how suddenly things can change or the alternative to not having your affairs completed, isn't it time to start? Choose to make an effort and not an excuse.

FAMILY DISCUSSION

Talking with family and loved ones is one of the most important tasks of planning your final affairs; sometimes, however, people may be reluctant to bring up these subjects. Not everyone likes to discuss money, finances, or death. They might feel it is not proper to discuss these topics. They may not want to "rock the boat" with their families or are afraid of hurting someone's feelings. Talking about the realization of when you will not be there may be difficult for some, while others may find these subjects too awkward or uncomfortable to bring up with their loved ones.

Family discussions about final affair areas can open the door for greater understanding while developing positive attitudes around these topics. Be gentle and patient with your loved ones. You may even find that the conversations can create or recall happy memories!

We all know a story where a death happens, and a family gets torn apart in the aftermath due to disagreements. Sometimes, while parents are alive, peace may be kept, situations and attitudes may be tolerated, but after someone's passing, emotions run high, and family issues are brought to light and are all too often compounded.

It's true; family dynamics can be crazy and complex, and some families simply do not get along. The complications of a blended family, addictions, toxic behavior, or other sensitive family issues are just a few examples of where tensions can arise. While you may not want to hurt anyone's feelings, all your careful planning won't see the light of day if people are arguing.

These sensitive issues will need to be addressed one way or another at some point. Doing it now allows you time to prepare for the conversations and to approach them logically, not emotionally. It gives you time to think of what you want to say and time to meet with family members in person. You can wait for the right moment, when people are in the right frame of mind. Discussions give you time to learn from each other's strengths. They allow for considerations, compromises, and time to find common ground.

A conversation should eliminate elements of surprise and reduce risks of disagreements. It can give you a chance to provide clarity about what you are doing and help family and friends understand why you believe your choices are the best course of action. These conversations are not meant to be uncomfortable or to make anyone scared. Make them casual, easy, and everyday conversations. Keep them light-hearted or add humor. You can have more minor discussions over a period of time, or you can host a sit-down and tell-all as a group or on a one-to-one basis.

No matter how you approach it, these discussions will allow you to express your wishes and intentions, while providing the opportunity to hear others' concerns. In addition, the conversations will help you to consider other options that might better suit you and your family. At the very least, talking will allow for questions and feedback that result in a better, more precise understanding for all involved.

WHO TO TALK TO AND WHAT TO TALK ABOUT

TALK TO YOUR SPOUSE/PARTNER

Ensure you know and understand each other's wishes and are willing to carry them out. Be sure both of you understand all final affair documentation and where papers, information, and assets are located. If this is not suitable, then identify someone you can trust to assist.

TALK TO YOUR FAMILY

Discuss your plans with your children, and, if appropriate, your grandchildren or any other close family or friend who will be impacted by your decisions. Where possible, include family in the planning process. Be certain they know what your wishes are, who you are choosing as Power of Attorney and Executor, and why.

TALK TO YOUR BENEFICIARIES

Discuss their inheritance, and why you are choosing this gift for them. You may discover they may not want or need the gift. A discussion also provides your beneficiaries the opportunity to express gratitude.

TALK TO YOUR POWER OF ATTORNEY AND EXECUTOR

Discuss their roles. Ensure the people you choose understand the work and time commitment that will be required. The people you choose may not have the availabilty or knowledge to take on these roles or would simply just rather not have the responsibility or obligation. Keep them updated when you make changes and most importantly, let them know where your papers are located!

These conversations may not be comfortable or easy, and unfortunately, there is no magic to make things easier; yet, it is important to make your wishes known. Be clear in what you say, explain where you are coming from and your reasons behind those decisions.

There are many on-line resources available to help begin the conversations and additional information can be found in many places, such as at your local library or bookstore, at funeral homes or care homes, or with estate lawyers or financial planners, just to name a few. Keep the people involved updated on a regular basis, and talk to your family. They will be the ones to deliver your objectives.

INFORMATION LOCATION AND UPKEEP

LOCATION

Final affair documents are very important. They are extremely helpful for the remaining spouse and are required for Power of Attorney and for Executors. These documents contain information only you know.

It is imperative to have this critical information gathered in one place. **Just in Case** suggests that you place all information for your final affairs in a binder, folder, filing cabinet, bank box, on a computer, or within **Just in Case**. If you save your information in other locations, be sure to reference those locations in one place. As well, if you save your information on your computer, guarantee all necessary passwords and folder locations are also included in **Just in Case** to allow for computer and file access.

Final affair documents contain sensitive, confidential, and high-risk information. Concern over the security of these documents is justified. People may be hesitant to keep all information in one place. To limit information theft, only disclose the location to those who require it. Follow your instincts. If you trust someone with your final affairs, you can trust them with the location of the papers. No one else is required to know where your papers are. Keep your information in a place that is out of sight, but can be located easily by the proper person when needed. When it comes to theft, typically thieves grab items that ensure a fast getaway, not papers located somewhere in a folder.

It can't be stated enough how essential it is to inform those who will be managing your affairs about the location of your final affair documentation. All your careful planning and preparation will go unused if no one knows about or is unable to locate your work.

KEEP IT UPDATED

Life constantly evolves. Families change, and people come and go. Births, deaths, marriages, and divorces are all a part of life. Situations and living arrangements can shift as people periodically move, start or finish school, get different jobs, or retire. In addition, information changes. You change banks, credit cards, passwords, insurance companies, brokers, lawyers, and accountants. Your assets change; for example, you purchase or sell vehicles or real estate or receive an inheritance.

Reflect about how much has happened in your life over the last year or two alone. Consider how much has changed with your household finances during the same time frame. (How many times have you changed your passwords?) Final affair areas can change that rapidly too. Unfortunately, it is not uncommon for people to have created a Will then not look at it for twenty or more years. It is safe to assume there has been at least one or two changes during that time!

Final affair documents are living documents; therefore, information must be reviewed regularly to maintain accuracy and relevance. Many of these papers or materials can be hard to find. Allow yourself time to review. Annually update information such as passwords, contact lists, health information, and financial information. Other documents, such as your Power of Attorney, your Last Will and Testament, Health Care Directive, and family history should be reviewed every three to five years or as recommended by your professional advisor. If you don't make formal arrangements, at the very least, write out your wishes to help your family.

HOW TO START (AND FINISH) PLANNING YOUR AFFAIRS

BREAK DOWN THE JOB

Advance planning your final affairs can be challenging. There is a lot to consider and a lot of ground to cover. The process can be lengthy and time-consuming. It is okay to take your time and work through the *Just in Case* final affair areas in small parts, section by section, and bit by bit. Remember, pre-planning allows for time, BUT it doesn't mean you should wait indefinitely! Set a date or block out time each week or month to work on it. This approach will not make the task feel so overwhelming, and you'll be surprised at the progress you will make.

ASK QUESTIONS

Don't be afraid to ask questions! Read through *Just in Case* and write down your questions. There are multiple free resources available on all subjects contained in *Just in Case*. Research topics on your computer or from resources at your local library. Ask someone you know or seek out professional assistance.

WORK WITH A PARTNER

Don't underestimate the power of experience! Sometimes it is better to have trusted family members or friends assist you with various sections.

WORK WITH YOUR SPOUSE/PARTNER

It is a great opportunity to ensure you understand each other's information. Don't assume you know!

WORK WITH A FAMILY MEMBER

It is a great learning and bonding experience. Different family members have various areas of expertise. For example, perhaps your daughter, a lawyer, can assist you with the legal sections. At the same time, your son, an accountant, can help you gather your financial information. Perhaps a grandchild could assist with recording your family history. It may give them the opportunity to learn things they never knew about your family!

WORK WITH YOUR FRIENDS

You may have friends or family members who have already gone through this process and might have answers to some of your questions. Ask them or others for tips and advice. Work with a friend who is also completing their affairs. Take someone with you to talk to a funeral home director. Perhaps you know someone who is in the medical field with whom you can discuss health care directives. Tap into these resources. Keep it light, friendly and fun!

WORK WITH YOUR POWER OF ATTORNEY OR EXECUTOR

Again, this is an excellent opportunity to discuss their roles and their required future tasks. Help them feel more prepared for when the time comes. It allows them time to ask questions and get clarification.

WORK WITH PROFESSIONALS

Go to someone who knows what they are doing! By seeking third-party assistance from a professional organization, such as a financial planner, a trust company, a law firm specializing in estate planning, or a final affair consultant, it will allow you to take the time to find the answers to your questions. They have the experience, expertise, and resources to guide you. It is what they do.

Money spent on professionals now may save even more money overall for you and your estate. It can eliminate the need for costly appointments when wishes are otherwise guessed at or are not known. The costs incurred now on professional appointments are far less than future court and legal charges when there are no plans or when legal documents are incorrectly created. Contact various professional organizations to see if they offer free brochures or seminars on these topics.

PART 2

FINAL AFFAIR CATEGORIES

NOTE: Each of the sections in Part 2 correspond to worksheets separated into sections at the back of this book. For example, Section 1 Personal Information corresponds to all worksheets beginning with the number 1. Worksheets begin on page 105.

Section 1
PERSONAL INFORMATION

Everyone assumes that your personal information is a given. Those closest to you should know who you are and where to find you; however, personal information for final affairs goes beyond name and contact information; and it involves a more in-depth approach. The data provided here is required by your Power of Attorney, Executors, health care professionals, people writing obituaries, or family members wanting to know history.

PERSONAL INFORMATION

To start, your personal information should have your current contact information, including your mobile number and your email address. Be sure to add your social insurance number, which is required to file your tax returns. Also, list your driver's licence number and location, date of birth, and your spouse or partner's name, etc.

MEDICAL INFORMATION

It is necessary to add medical information as it may be required for many situations, including medical assistance, communicating your medical history when you are unable, or determining your family medical history. Be sure to include things like your provincial health number or card, a list of all your physicians and specialists, your medical history with dates, any known allergies, a list of current and past medications, your pharmacist, your blood type, and if you are an organ donor. The more detailed you are here, the better. Be sure to use straightforward language to eliminate any interpretation issues.

MILITARY SERVICE

Serving in the military under any capacity is an honorable commitment and should be recognized. Listing your rank, unit, and branch, along with locations of service and associated dates, is a wonderful legacy to leave your family members. Adding your own personal stories to this information is an added treasure!

TECHNOLOGY

There are many technological services and programs that we use every day. Documenting what you use is very helpful to someone who will be required to have access when you are unable to.

List your devices and the locations where they are typically kept, along with usernames and passwords. Include any devices used for work purposes as well.

As our world becomes increasingly more technologically advanced, online services consistantly increase. Keep a list of all online services you subscribe to, along with all usernames and passwords. Include services like Facebook, Instagram, Google, Microsoft, Amazon, Apple, Hotmail, etc. Remember, your passwords change all the time! Please review the list annually to maintain accuracy.

LEGAL INFORMATION

Write down the name and contact information for your lawyer and law firm. Be sure to indicate the type of practice (family law, real estate, etc.) and the purpose of the relationship or reason for services. Include any other information, such as dates, that may be relevant.

EDUCATION

Where and when did you go to school? Did you attend post-secondary school? Did you receive a diploma or certificate? Your education information could be of interest to those creating obituaries or to curious family members.

COMBINATIONS AND CODES

This is an excellent place to capture the combinations and codes for any safe, locks, alarms or door openers. Be sure to include their locations and a list of people who also know these combinations or codes. Access to your property and possessions is required by your Executor and possibly your Power of Attorney. If your house is protected by a security service it is important to understand the requirements in the event of the death of the home owner. It may be wise to give your security service provider the names of your Power of Attorney and Executor.

MEMBERSHIPS, REGISTRATIONS, ETC.

Are you a member of a social organization? Do you play with a sports team? Do you have a membership at a gym, a store or at your local library? Do you subscribe to any publications? Do you have registrations for jewelry or for firearms? Do you have a post office box? Be sure to capture required information here to notify, change or cancel any of the above.

OTHER INFORMATION

Finally, enclose any other information that may not be listed. Be sure to read through *Just in Case*, as it may be included elsewhere in this book.

SUMMARY

As you can see, the Personal Information section is quite detailed. Include all you know and update it regularly to maintain accuracy. Your family will be grateful for your efforts.

Happy listing!

Section 2
CONTACT LISTS

I n critical situations, there are people and organizations who need to be notified. Usually, at these difficult times, there are heavy emotions, and loved ones are often under stress or in grief as they scramble to figure out who to contact. Something as easy as finding a phone number or an email address can become a challenging task, and people can be forgotten. Keeping a list of who should be notified and how to connect with them will assist those who are looking after your affairs.

Review these contact lists annually as information changes over time. Include phone numbers, email addresses and any other notes that may be applicable.

PERSONAL

List family and friends who should be contacted immediately by phone, email or text message… just in case something happens. These people are to be contacted in case of emergency, death, or should be the first to know.

- Include name, phone number, address, email, and your relationship with the contact. Include a work contact if applicable.

- Indicate if this person is the start of a contact chain. This is when one person is responsible for contacting other family members or friends. For example, your sister would be responsible for notifying your side of the family, and your son is responsible for notifying your spouse's family. Ensure that the person who will be responsible for a chain knows the current contact information.

- In times of death or emergency, there may also be many acts or gifts of kindness, including flowers, food and visits. Express thanks and appreciation with a phone call, card, email or message when possible.

GOVERNMENT, BUSINESSES, AND ORGANIZATIONS

GOVERNMENT AGENCIES

There are certain government departments and registries that require notification when major changes occur, such as Power of Attorney coming into effect, death, a name change, etc.

ORGANIZATIONS AND MEMBERSHIPS

List benefit companies, professional or business organizations, board memberships or others that will require notification. Also, include any social, sport or charitable organization where you are a member. These include things like clubs, fraternities/sororities, churches or community organizations. This is also a good place to list any subscriptions, such as retail reward programs.

SERVICES AND BUSINESSES

Include businesses that provide personal services for you or your residence, such as estheticians, yard care services, home cleaning services, etc; any place where future appointments have been made.

Section 3
FINANCIAL INFORMATION

T he details in this section are vital, as they will be required for your Power of Attorney, Executor and surviving spouse/partner. **Be certain that the people filling these roles know where this information is.**

This information will also be required by your lawyer prior to creating a Will. Having this material compiled before a legal meeting, may save you time and money.

This section takes a lot of work. It will involve searching, as most people have this data in various places. You will be making many lists, and identifying where items are, including physical locations. You will be providing contact information, passwords, PIN numbers, as well as other details that only you know.

It is essential these documents be kept in one location to make less work for your surviving spouse or partner, your Power of Attorney and/or your Executor. Put all information within *Just in Case* or please indicate in your final affair papers where the information or documents can be found.

ACCOUNTANT

Who does your income tax? Have you done estate tax planning? Where is your property tax information?

Your accounting information will be required by your estate to complete a final income tax return. Please ensure your accountant's contact information is included, while also indicating the accountant's specialty (general, tax, business, etc.).

FINANCIAL PLANNER

Do you have RRSPs, RIFs, or investments? Do you understand capital gains? Do you have beneficiaries listed for your investments? Do you have family trusts? Do you own a business or a farm? Have you completed succession planning?

List your financial planner's name and firm, along with contact information. Be sure to provide copies of your investment portfolios, any broker orders, or share certificates.

FINANCIAL/BANKING INSTITUTIONS

Sometimes people use more than one financial institution. Perhaps your mortgage is at one bank, a car loan is with a separate bank, and your day-to-day banking is at yet another. Be sure to list each institution's name and the location of the branches. Include account numbers, their approximate balances, and how they are used. (For example: Chequing Account xxx-xxx: used for daily banking; Savings Account xxx-xxx: used for travel savings.) List any automatic withdrawals from these accounts, debit and credit cards with PIN and passwords, and safety deposit box information, along with a list of contents and key location.

It is necessary to understand the rights of survivorship for joint accounts. Talk with your bank to determine the availability of banking funds upon death; some accounts may be frozen for a time. It is also a good practice to know how much income a survivor will require for the immediate month or two following the death of a spouse/partner to cover daily living costs, and be certain these funds can be accessed.

INCOME

Are you employed? If so, what is your salary and how often are you paid? Do you have other income? Business revenues? If you are retired, what is your source of income? Do you have pensions? Where and how is your income deposited? Understand what happens to these income sources if Power of Attorney begins or when a death occurs.

MORTGAGE, LOANS AND OTHER LIABILITIES

Provide information regarding your loans and mortgages, including the approximate values, lending institutions, account numbers, interest rates, maturity dates, etc. Include any joint liability with another partner. List any contractual obligations you may have, including child support, alimony, garnishee or court order, and provide as many details as possible.

MAJOR ASSETS

Prepare an inventory of all major assets with their approximate value and full particulars. Include title documentation. Please indicate, where applicable, what major assets are included in your Will.

Businesses and Holdings

If a company is owned, please discuss succession planning with a lawyer, accountant, and other necessary professionals and individuals. While recording the company and holdings within *Just in Case*, be sure to indicate where succession documentation can be located.

Real Estate and Property

Include home, cottage, farmland, out of country residences, etc. Indicate legal property address or land location (if applicable), names on the registration, if a property is owned outright or if it is mortgaged, and the estimated or appraised current market value. Also, enclose in this section any owned vehicles and recreational vehicles. Include their location, if the vehicle is owned or leased, and the estimated current market value.

Lease Agreements

List the company, institution or individuals that hold the lease agreement, and note the lease terms. Be sure to include a copy of the lease with your documentation.

INSURANCE POLICIES

Indicate all insurance policies, including: life, accidental, disability, medical, house, property, vacation home, vehicle, recreational vehicles, etc. Include policy information, premium, coverage amount, and payment dates and any beneficiaries if applicable.

UTILITIES

This is a great place to indicate your monthly utilities. Detail account information, names on the account, approximate monthly charge, and how the utility is paid.

SUMMARY

Over time, the details and documents in this section will continue to change. It is critical to review these items annually to make any necessary adjustments. The more detailed you can be, the better. Take it slowly. Review and insert your material as it comes to you throughout the year. Please remember that the information in this section is necessary for your surviving spouse, Power of Attorney, and your Executor.

Section 4
POWER OF ATTORNEY

Once you have decided who will act as your Power of Attorney, discuss the role and duties with your chosen person(s). Be sure they know the location of your final affair documentation, as it contains all data required to perform these duties. It is also an excellent idea to let your loved ones know who your Power of Attorney is to ensure he or she can be called upon when necessary.

TERMINOLOGY

Grantor: You - the person appointing another to act on your behalf.

Attorney: The person you give the power to act on your behalf for your personal and property affairs.

Enduring Power of Attorney: This type of Power of Attorney remains in effect, even if the person granting the power (Grantor) becomes incapacitated.

Specific Power of Attorney: This type of Power of Attorney limits the authority to a particular purpose (e.g., sale of property on a grantor's behalf).

WHAT IS POWER OF ATTORNEY?

Power of Attorney is a document that appoints another person to act on your behalf for your personal and property affairs. A Power of Attorney has the legal authority to do any task that you are legally able to do.

WHY IS POWER OF ATTORNEY IMPORTANT?

- Having a Power of Attorney allows you to choose who will manage your personal and property affairs for a specific or extended time period.

- It helps you plan for a time when you may not be able to make decisions.

- It can provide peace of mind for yourself and those you care about.

WHAT ARE THE DUTIES OF A POWER OF ATTORNEY?

Power of Attorneys are required to:

- Act honestly.

- Act in good faith.

- Act in the best interests of the Grantor.

- Take the Grantor's wishes into consideration while carrying out all duties on their behalf.

- Unless there are restrictions, the Power of Attorney is allowed to do the following on the Grantor's behalf:

    - Open and close bank accounts.
    - Redirect pensions and other income.
    - Apply for benefits or supplementary income to which the person is entitled.
    - Choose pension options.
    - Deal with investments.
    - Collect debts.
    - Pay bills.
    - Buy goods and services, real property and real estate.
    - Start or defend lawsuits if there are financial implications.
    - Sell, store, or dispose of personal belongings.

- Maintain or sell a house or vehicle.
- Give gifts on the Grantor's behalf.

WHAT CAN'T A POWER OF ATTORNEY DO?

A Power of Attorney cannot:

- Change the Grantor's Will or make a new one.

- Give gifts larger than the prescribed amount, which is currently $1,000 in total for all gifts per year, unless authorized by the court.

- Assume ownership of the Grantor's income and assets. Ownership remains in the name of the Grantor.

WHO CAN QUALIFY AS A POWER OF ATTORNEY?

- Someone who is 18 years of age or older.

- They must be mentally competent.

- It can be an individual or a corporation.

- It does not have to be a lawyer.

- It can be a family member, friend, or another person.

- They can live in a different province from the Grantor; however, it is advised that you use someone local for ease and provincial law understanding.

WHO CANNOT BE A POWER OF ATTORNEY?

- Someone who is in undischarged bankruptcy (in the case of property attorney).

- Someone who has been convicted within the last ten years of a Criminal Code Offence for an act of violence, theft, fraud, or breach of trust.

- Someone who is in the business of providing personal or health care services to the Grantor for compensation.

CAN I HAVE MORE THAN ONE POWER OF ATTORNEY?

- You can appoint more than one Power of Attorney and give specific powers to each.

- They can act **separately**: Each act individually with different duties.

- They can act **together (jointly)**: The Powers of Attorney must decide and act together.
- They can act **successively**: The first person listed serves. If the first person can't or won't fulfill the role, the next becomes authorized to serve.

* Unless stated, it is assumed that two or more appointed attorneys are to act jointly and their decisions must be unanimous.

WHAT IS A CORPORATE POWER OF ATTORNEY?

If you don't know anyone who would fit the role of Power of Attorney, or you do not wish to burden anyone with this role; then, consider having a professional act on your behalf.

Examples of Corporate Powers of Attorney are trust companies, lawyers, or financial institutions. A corporate Power of Attorney must disclose their fees in writing to the Grantor before signing an enduring Power of Attorney.

WHAT IS AN ENDURING POWER OF ATTORNEY?

An Enduring Power of Attorney is a Power of Attorney that continues in effect even if the Grantor becomes incapacitated. There are two types of Enduring Power of Attorney. You can indicate which you choose when drafting the Power of Attorney document.

Immediate Enduring Power of Attorney

This Power of Attorney comes into effect immediately.

Contingent or "Springing" Power of Attorney

This Power of Attorney comes into effect on a **specified future date**. (e.g., a Grantor leaving the country for an extended period) or for a **specific event** (e.g., when a Grantor becomes mentally incapacitated).

WHAT ARE THE DIFFERENT TYPES OF POWER OF ATTORNEY?

There are two types:

1. **General Power of Attorney**: Covers all the Grantor's personal affairs (Personal Power of Attorney) or all of their property affairs (Property Power of Attorney) or both. See below for further definition of these roles.

2. **Limited or Specific Power of Attorney**: This type limits the Power of Attorney's

authority to a specific purpose, such as selling a property on the Grantor's behalf.

General PROPERTY Power of Attorney

A Property Power of Attorney can arrange your business, property and financial affairs, including paying your bills, filing your taxes, representing your interests in court, changing your land titles, or managing your investments; however, they cannot make or change a Will for you.

What qualities should I look for in my Power of Attorney for Property?

- **Trustworthy**: These people should have a financially clean slate when entrusted with others' finances. They should not be desperate for money.

- **Capable**: The Power of Attorney should know how to arrange your affairs in addition to their own. They should be able to get things done in the business world.

- **Accountable**: They should readily share information about what they are doing and disclose any fees they might charge for doing their work.

General PERSONAL Power of Attorney

A Personal Power of Attorney looks after all personal affairs of the Grantor, including, but not limited to: health care, food, clothing, shelter, personal hygiene, and cultural or religious needs. For example, they may help to decide where you should live, who should do your hair, who might assist with travel, etc.

They **do not** make Healthcare Directive decisions, such as Do Not Resuscitate, and cannot arrange financial payments.

What qualities should I look for in my personal Power of Attorney?

- **Attentive**: Someone who knows you and the way you live. They understand your preferences. They will look out for your personal needs and make arrangements for your care, lifestyle, and cultural needs.

- **Available**: Someone who lives close is preferred. They should be able to come to help when called upon.

General Power of Attorney for both Personal and Property Affairs

Most Enduring Power of Attorney documents name someone to serve as both Property and Personal Power of Attorney. There are cases, however, where one person may not be suitable to serve in both roles.

For example, a grandchild might be a good choice for your Personal Power of Attorney, but they may not have the skills to deal with financial matters. Meanwhile, another relative, or perhaps a professional trust company, might be better suited to fit the role of Property Power of Attorney. It is essential to have the people with the right skill set and availability for these roles.

WHAT ARE THE LEGAL REQUIREMENTS FOR CREATING A POWER OF ATTORNEY?

- You, the Grantor, must have mental competency.

- You, the Grantor, must be at least 18 years old.

- It must be done in writing.

- Must be signed and dated by the Grantor.

- Must be witnessed by a lawyer and accompanied by a Legal Advice Certificate or witnessed by two competent adults and accompanied by two Witness Certificates.

- Witnesses cannot be the named Power of Attorney nor can family members of either the Grantor or family members of named Powers of Attorney.

- Check with provincial laws regarding recognizing Power of Attorney made outside of the province. Generally, if the Power of Attorney is valid according to the law of the province it was created, it is acceptable.

CAN I CREATE POWER OF ATTORNEY WITHOUT A LAWYER?

Power of Attorney is one of the most powerful roles an individual can have. Unfortunately, there are those who abuse this power. For this reason, **it is strongly advised that you create a Power of Attorney using the legal advice of a lawyer.**

You can, however, create a Power of Attorney without a lawyer. To do this, you must use approved forms according to your province, which can be found on most provincial government websites.

DOES A POWER OF ATTORNEY GET PAID?

This role is very time-consuming and work intensive. A Power of Attorney is entitled to the following compensation:

- A Property Attorney can collect a fee based on a percentage of all money received and all money paid by the property attorney.

- Personal Attorneys are entitled to receive a per hour fee for the time spent on the Grantor's personal affairs.

- A Grantor may decide a fee of their choosing and indicate this fee within the Power of Attorney document.

- A court may also set Power of Attorney fees.

HOW IS ACCOUNTING HANDLED?

Powers of Attorney should keep careful records of all transactions involving the property of the Grantor. A list of records to be tracked and certain accounting forms are outlined by and available from most provincial governments.

- The Power of Attorney may be required to submit accounts to court for inspection.

- The Power of Attorney is required to account to the Grantor whenever the Grantor asks.

- A Power of Attorney who charges a fee must provide accounting annually.

- The Power of Attorney must retain the accounts and records until such time as:
  - they are no longer acting as Power of Attorney;
  - the courts have approved the accounts;
  - they have been provided with a release signed by the Grantor or a legal representative of the Grantor.
- The Power of Attorney must provide a final accounting form from the provincial government when the Power of Attorney is revoked, or the Grantor dies. This form is given to the Executor or any new decision-maker.

HOW DO I END A POWER OF ATTORNEY?

A Power of Attorney can end in the following ways:

- It can be revoked by the Grantor.

- A specific date of completion can be listed within the Power of Attorney document.

- It must be in writing (include the words "Notice of Revocation").

- It must be signed and dated.

- A witness is not required but preferred.

- Creating a new Power of Attorney does NOT cancel any previous Power of Attorney. Be clear if you are revoking a previous Power of Attorney.

- A copy shall be given to each Power of Attorney identified (Registered mail).
- If the Power of Attorney is no longer able or willing to act, they may resign.

SUMMARY

Power of Attorney DOs

- DO seek legal advice when determining Power of Attorney. Power of Attorney abuse is quite common; however, it can be avoided with the proper documentation and wording for which a professional provides.
- DO give careful thought to the person you choose.
- DO talk to the person you choose before you sign.
- DO keep a copy of your Power of Attorney documentation with your final affair arrangements and with those named as your Power of Attorney.
- DO inform those who need to know (lawyer, bank, family) once the Power of Attorney is signed.

Power of Attorney DON'Ts

- DON'T sign without getting legal advice.
- DON'T sign under pressure or duress (if you are unsure).
- DON'T name someone you cannot trust or who isn't a good money manager.

Section 5
HEALTH CARE DIRECTIVE

WHAT IS A HEALTH CARE DIRECTIVE?

- It is a document, prepared in advance, that contains your wishes concerning medical treatment, for when you can no longer communicate these decisions for yourself.

- Sometimes referred to as a Living Will.

- It is also for consideration of organ and tissue donations.

WHAT DOES A DIRECTIVE DO?

- It is a document that gives your doctor or health care provider directions about what kind of measures are acceptable to you when you can no longer communicate what you want.

- It is for your right to consent or to refuse direct treatment.

- This document gives your doctor or health care provider protection from legal action if they follow the directive.
- A directive CANNOT permit medically assisted dying.

WHO CAN MAKE A DIRECTIVE?

To create a Health Care Directive a person must be:

- 16 years of age.
- Capable of making heath care decisions (able to understand information about potential treatments and the consequences of making or not making a decision).
- Able to communicate decisions.

WHEN SHOULD I MAKE A DIRECTIVE?

- If you know you are ill.
- If you are currently in good health but are planning for a time when you can no longer make decisions for yourself.

HOW DOES INCAPACITY AFFECT A DIRECTIVE?

If you are considered incapacitated, it is too late to make a Health Care Directive.

A Personal Power of Attorney dealing with your personal affairs cannot make decisions on treatments, end of life decisions, or other matters captured in a Health Care Directive.

WHAT ARE THE REQUIREMENTS FOR CREATING A DIRECTIVE?

The following are requirements for making a Health Care Directive:

- It must be in writing (handwritten or typed).
- It must have your signature and date.
- If you sign it yourself, it does not have to be witnessed.
- If you are unable to sign the directive yourself, your signature must be witnessed by another person other than your Proxy or your Proxy's spouse.
- You must be over the age of 16.

- You must be mentally capable.
- The Directive must be brought to the attention of health care providers.
- There is no official form, but some agencies, such as hospitals or medical offices, have forms or samples to use as a guide. A Health Care Directive can also be created with your estate lawyer.

WHAT SHOULD BE INCLUDED IN A DIRECTIVE?

- Specific instructions regarding certain treatments and situations (e.g.: Do Not Resuscitate).
- Be as clear and as straight forward as possible. Health care providers do not have to follow directions that are not coherent.

WHEN DOES A DIRECTIVE TAKE EFFECT?

- A Directive will take effect when you become incapable of making or communicating your health care decisions.

HOW DO I CANCEL A DIRECTIVE?

- Directives can be cancelled orally or in writing.
- Destroy old Directives.
- Making a new Directive will cancel the old Directive.

WHAT IS A PROXY?

- A Proxy is a person who has the authority to represent someone else.
- A Proxy can make all or some of the health care decisions for you when you are not able to make or communicate those decisions yourself or when your Directive does not address the situation.

WHO CAN BE A PROXY?

A Proxy:

- Must be at least 18 years old.
- Must have the capacity to make health care decisions.

- Does not have to be a family member.

WHAT SHOULD I CONSIDER WHEN NAMING A PROXY?

- Name someone you trust.

- You may name two or more Proxies if you wish.

- If you appoint two or more Proxies they can act as alternate or joint Proxies.

- If you name your spouse and later divorce, the appointment will be revoked unless you state in your Directive that the appointment will continue after your divorce.

- A Proxy can decline the position, but they cannot pass this responsibility to another person.

- Be certain that the person you name can follow through with your wishes when the time comes, as this can be a highly emotional task.

- Be sure your Proxy can withstand conflicting opinions from other family members.

HOW DOES A PROXY MAKE DECISIONS?

- Decisions must be made in accordance with the wishes set out in the Health Care Directive.

- Treatment wishes should be discussed clearly and completely with your Proxy. If they know your wishes, they must act accordingly.

- If the Proxy does not know your wishes, or if no specific wishes are expressed in the Health Care Directive, then decisions must be in accordance with:

  - Any verbal wishes expressed while you were still competent.
  - Recent decisions made while still competent.
  - If no direction has been provided, then they must act according to what they believe is in your best interests.

WHAT HAPPENS IF THERE ARE DISPUTES?

If a dispute arises, an interested person may apply to court to challenge the appointment of a Proxy, or a decision made by a Proxy or nearest relative.

WHAT HAPPENS IF I DO NOT HAVE A HEALTH CARE DIRECTIVE?

If you do not have a Health Care Directive prepared, your next of kin, based on legislation, will make the decisions on your behalf. Legal next of kin is determined by the health care provider in the following order, including cases of adoption:

- Spouse or person you live with as a spouse

- Adult child

- Parent or legal custodian

- Adult sibling

- Grandparent

- Adult grandchild

- Adult uncle or aunt

- Adult niece or nephew

The decision of a relative of whole blood is preferred over the decision of a relative of half-blood. If there is more than one person in the same category, the decision of the eldest will be preferred. The decision of a custodial parent will be preferred over the decision of a non-custodial parent. If there are no family members, or family members cannot be found, then your doctor or other healthcare provider will make a decision for you by consulting another doctor or health care provider. The second doctor must agree in writing that the proposed treatment is needed.

SUMMARY

Health Care Directives DOs

- DO talk about your wishes with your Proxy and your family. Confirm their understanding of your preferences and their willingness to follow through.

- DO give copies of your Directive to your Proxy, physician, and family, if appropriate.

- DO talk to your physician if you intend to include statements about treatment.

- DO use clear and concise language when expressing your wishes.

Health Care Directives DON'Ts

- DON'T put the only copy in your safety deposit box or anywhere it cannot be found.

- DON'T keep it a secret.

- DON'T use 'legalese' or 'jargon' when expressing your choices.

Section 6
WILL AND ESTATE
INFORMATION

A Will is the most recognized area of final affair planning. It is also the document most people are afraid of starting. It includes unfamiliar legal language, and the process can be intimidating and overwhelming.

This chapter is all about education. It is often helpful to understand the requirements for creating a Will and the process of estate administration to help identify any potential areas of concern for your estate and your loved ones.

A Will is an essential document, and it is critical to have it created properly. *Just in Case* strongly recommends the use of an estate lawyer. If a last Will and Testament is not legally or correctly drawn up, the results may cause turmoil. It could result in costly and lengthy court battles and, in some cases, tear people and families apart. Please read through each section carefully to understand the complete process of Will creation and consider the specific requirements or suggestions.

Settle in. This is a long chapter. There is a lot to cover when talking about Wills and Estates. Take it slow and easy. First, become familiar with the language in the Terminology section. We'll then talk about choosing an Executor and the responsibilities of an Executor, to ensure you select the right person to manage these duties. We'll then look at what is necessary for creating a Will and finish off with describing estate administration, while including a couple of checklists for both the loved one's survivors and the Executors.

Ready?

Here we go.

6.1 TERMINOLOGY

Administrator: Sometimes used in place of either Executor or Executrix. This court-appointed person manages the estate if the testator (the person who makes a Will) does not name an Executor in their Will or when no Will exists.

Beneficiary: A person named in a Will to receive some part of the estate.

Bequest: A gift, usually of personal property, under a Will.

Codicil: An addition or change to a Will.

Devise: A gift or transfer of real property under a Will.

Estate: All assets and liabilities of the deceased that make up their estate. These include all personal possessions and real property.

Executor: A person named in a Will to carry out the terms of the Will. An Executor is a person who will have the legal responsibility to settle your estate after your death. It is the more commonly used term these days for any individual who serves in this capacity, even when she's a woman.

Executrix: Sometimes used to describe a female Executor, but this term is not used often anymore.

Holographic Will: A Will written and signed entirely in a testator's own hand and unsigned by any witnesses.

Intestate: When a person dies without a Will.

Personal Property: Refers to goods and money, including furniture, vehicles, jewelry, animals, clothing, stocks, shares, patents, and copyrights.

Personal Representative: Sometimes used in place of either Executor or Executrix.

Probate: The court process of proving that a Will is valid and administering the estate under the supervision of the courts.

Probate Letters or Letters of Administration: Documents issued by the court authorizing an Executor or an administrator to deal with an estate.

Real Property: Refers to immovable property such as land and real estate.

Residue: Property remaining after specific items are distributed in a Will.

Rights of Survivorship: When real property is owned jointly with another person or other people and one joint owner dies, ownership of property transfers directly to the surviving joint owner(s).

Spouse: A person who is married to the testator or who has lived together with the testator as a spouse for two or more years. *Please note that this legal definition can vary based on jurisdiction. Please consult the provincial law in your location.

Testator: The person who makes a Will.

Testatrix: Sometimes used to describe a female testator.

6.2 CHOOSING AN EXECUTOR

It is advised to keep your Executor informed about your Will regularly to ensure complete understanding of your decisions and the location of recorded information (your final affair documentation). Doing so will hopefully reduce administration time or later conflict.

WHAT IS AN EXECUTOR?

An Executor is a person named in a Will to carry out the terms of the Will. An Executor is the person who will have the legal responsibility to settle your estate after your death.

WHEN DOES AN EXECUTOR START THEIR DUTIES?

Executor duties start immediately upon death.

HOW LONG IS THE EXECUTOR'S POSITION?

The job of the Executor will continue until the estate is settled. **Settling an estate takes anywhere from 18 months to several years, depending on the size of the estate or the complexity.** Some factors that can prolong settling an estate are: if the estate has business assets, challenging family dynamics or members, a highly valuable estate, a low-value estate, unforeseen issues, or if the Executor does not have the time, health, interest, skill set, or ability to efficiently settle your estate.

WHO MAKES AN IDEAL EXECUTOR?

Having the right Executor can make a big difference in estate settlement. The following are some characteristics of the ideal Executor:

- Choose a responsible, trustworthy, and competent person.

- It is preferable to have an Executor who lives in your province; it is more convenient and less costly. If your Executor does not live in the same area as you, it can be challenging but not impossible to manage the assets and issues from a distance.

- Someone who has experience managing money and dealing with financial institutions.

- Someone who can deal with your relatives and beneficiaries objectively.

- Someone comfortable dealing with lawyers and accountants.

- Someone who has the time to settle your estate, which may be equivalent to a part-time job for approximately one and a half to two years.

- An Executor should have patience to deal with government agencies, such as tax departments.

- A person who is organized and willing to do lots of paperwork.

- A person who is not afraid to ask for professional help when needed.

- Someone who has experience settling estates or who is willing to read, research, and learn about estate settlement.

- If you are over the age of sixty, it is preferable to have an Executor who is younger than you.

CAN MY PARTNER, FAMILY MEMBER, FRIEND, OR BENEFICIARY BE MY EXECUTOR?

- Married people will often choose each other as their Executor. This may be a good idea if the Will states that the sole beneficiary is the surviving spouse. This may not be a good idea if the spouse is elderly, unhealthy, or financially inexperienced. As well, it may be best to choose another Executor if there are multiple beneficiaries, if the deceased has had more than one marriage, if there are children from different unions, or if challenging family situations exist.

- The Executor can be a beneficiary.

- If you plan to use a friend or a family member as your Executor, discuss the role before creating the Will. They may not want to take on the responsibility, which can hold up the distribution of the estate, and people have the right to refuse this position.

HOW MANY EXECUTORS SHOULD I HAVE?

The number of Executors you have is really a personal choice. When making this decision, consider the following: if you have one person, it is recommended to also have an Alternate Executor as back up in case the first is unable or unwilling to act, but having more than one means that they must be accountable to each other. (More than two Executors make estate administration more complicated.)

WHAT ARE THE DIFFERENT TYPES OF EXECUTORS?

Sole Executor: An individual named in your Will who acts alone in the Executor role.

Alternate Executor: A person named in your Will who will execute the role of Executor, in case the first named Executor (called Primary Executor) cannot act. You can name one or more Alternate Executors. Again, it is suggested to have at least one Alternate Executor if your Primary Executor is unable or unwilling to act.

Co-Executors: An individual can name more than one Executor to act as **Co-Executors**. These may also be called **Joint Executors**.

> *Important note:*
>
> ***All executors have <u>full</u> authority over the estate and are responsible for <u>every</u> aspect of the estate.***

- <u>All</u> Executors must collaborate on all matters including decision making, and information sharing in estate administration. **<u>All</u> decisions must be unanimous.**

- All Executors must perform certain duties together. A couple of examples would be: submitting the Will for probate or signing documents and cheques on behalf of the estate.

WHAT ARE THE BENEFITS OF CO-EXECUTORS?

- Distribution of an estate in a fair and honest manner.

- Shared duties and responsibilities of estate administration.

- Different skills and knowledge.

- Each Executor can be responsible for different areas of the estate. For example, one may sell real estate, while another may distribute the goods within the house. Caution: Even if Co-Executors oversee different areas of the estate, ALL Executors are fully responsible for ALL aspects of the estate.

WHAT ARE THE DISADVANTAGES OF CO-EXECUTORS?

- If decisions are not unanimous, disagreements must be settled in court.

- Logistics and time, especially if the Co-Executors do not live in proximity of each other.

- Confusion and misinterpretation between Executors.

- Estate administration may become more complex.

- Each Co-Executor is responsible for the other's actions, even if duties are not performed together. This means if one Executor commits an illegal act while settling the estate, the other joint-Excecutor is also responsible for this same act.

- One Co-Executor may refuse to serve or be slower with administration, which can stall the process.

- If Co-Executors are family, it may cause stress on these relationships.

CAN ESTATE AND TRUST COMPANIES HELP?

Sometimes you don't have the right person to take on this role in your life. Perhaps you feel like your named Executor may need some assistance. Maybe naming a family member or close friend will cause issues. In these cases, and many others, it might be helpful to use an estate and trust company either as a Sole Executor, Co-Executor, or Alternate Executor.

Sole Executor Services: An estate and trust company is appointed in a Will to act independently to conduct your wishes.

This is ideal for individuals who:

- Have no family or friends to function as Executor.

- Are struggling with a challenging family situation.

- Are not sure who to appoint as the Executor for their estate.

- Prefer that an objective professional handles everything.

- Feel that the administration of your estate is too complex or too time consuming for family or friends.

Co-Executor Services: An estate and trust company is appointed in a Will to act alongside another individual you name to carry out your wishes. This professional Co-Executor ensures a solid degree of competence and experience, which is especially important if substantial assets are involved or if trusts are to be administered.

This is ideal for individuals who:

- Want a close friend or family member involved to make decisions, but don't want to burden them with heavy administrative tasks.

- Prefer that a professional handle all the technical aspects of estate administration.

- Are struggling with a challenging family situation.

Alternate Executor Services: Estate or trust companies can also function as an alternate Executor if the original Executor is unwilling or unable to fulfill their responsibilities.

Agent for Executor Services: Estate or trust companies can aid named Executors by handling some or all of the Executor's duties. The named Executor ultimately makes all the final decisions.

Executor Services are ideal for individuals who:

- Are now filling the Executor role.

- Need assistance with certain areas of their duties.

- Find their family situation challenging and need the sensitivity and expertise of an impartial third party.

- Lack the time, expertise, or desire to administer an estate.

- Live outside the city, province, or country where the estate is located.

- Want to retain final decision-making authority while benefiting from professional expertise.

WHAT ARE EXECUTOR/ADMINISTRATOR DUTIES?

Some of the duties are as follows: (For a more detailed list, please see the Estate Administration section on page 69 or the Executor Checklist on page 65.)

- Publish an obituary.

- Publish a Notice to Creditors in the local paper to protect the estate from liability.

- Locate or determine if there is a Will.

- Distribute the estate according to the Will.

- Locate all assets of the deceased and determine their value.

- Obtain a death certificate.

- Notify various agencies of the death. (A copy of the death certificate may be required.)

- Create a list of all beneficiaries, including addresses.

- File life insurance claims, pension plans, and other death benefits.

- Pay funeral bills.

- Obtain appropriate Court Orders, Letters Probate or Letters of Administration.

- If there are children under the age of 18 or if there are dependant adults, notify the Public Guardian and Trustee.

- Call in the estate: gather assets, arrange for sale or distribution of assets not specifically left to a beneficiary, and place all money into an estate bank account.

- Transfer title for all real property to the estate.

- Pay bills and debts of the deceased and the estate.

- Complete Income Tax Returns and obtain the Income Tax Clearance Certificate required to complete the estate distribution.

- Keep records of assets coming into and going out of the estate.

- Obtain releases from beneficiaries required to complete the distribution of the estate.

- Arrange for the passing of accounts if there are disputes between the beneficiaries (asking the court to approve your financial records of the estate and your plan for estate distribution).

DOES AN EXECUTOR GET PAID?

Anyone who settles your estate is entitled to be paid. Again, remember that this position can be equivalent to a part-time job for approximately one and a half to two years. Executors are entitled to a fair and reasonable allowance. Alternatively, at times the Executor may waive the payment. **The Executor fees must be agreed upon with the consent of all beneficiaries.**

There is no actual set amount for Executor fees but consider the following:

- Size of the estate, the amount of work the Executor manages, and the difficulty of the estate.

- Responsibility involved.

- Time occupied.

- Skill required.

- Success achieved.

Compensation is sometimes calculated on a percentage based on money that passes through an estate, and Executor fees are usually between 1% - 5% of the estate value. This number should be used as a guideline and not a determining factor.

Even if you state your Executor fee in your Will, be aware that your Executor can seek the approval of a court to be paid more. A Will with a fixed or specific fee for Executor services cannot provide additional reimbursement for expenses the Executor may encounter while fulfilling their role. **Please discuss Executor fees with an estate lawyer.**

Trust and Estate Company Fees: These organizations charge fees to administer the estate. The agreed upon fees are charged to your estate, and they are usually a percentage of your estate on a sliding scale (the larger the estate, the smaller the percentage fee); they typically start around 3 - 5% on the first $1 million in your estate. Trust companies, like any Executor, will also demand repayment of expenses incurred on the estate's behalf (for example, legal fees, accounting fees, and realtor fees).

WHAT INFORMATION SHOULD I HAVE FOR MY EXECUTOR?

Your Executor will require most of the information found within *Just in Case*.

The documentation should be gathered in one location, and the Executor is made aware of that location. At minimum, it is vital to ensure exact document location is listed in one place. Safeguard original copies. Notarized or True Copies made from the original documents may be required.

A list of required documents for your Executor includes, but is not limited to, the following:

- Last Will and Testament. (A notarized copy will be required in most situations.)
- Law firm and/or lawyer who created your Will and who your Executor can use for legal advice if necessary.
- Contact names and information for financial and tax advice.
- Contact lists of family and friends who will require notification.
- Funeral and burial arrangements.
- All financial information, including major assets and liabilities.
- Proof of Earnings (current and previous year) - required for Death Benefit.
- Life insurance policies.
- Instructions concerning different matters relating to your estate.
- Titles to real estate property - include home, farmland, cottage, or out-of-country residence.
- Birth certificate, baptismal certificate, marriage certificate, divorce certificate, etc.
- Social Insurance Number.
- Credit/Debit Cards - These need to be cancelled immediately.
- Passport - The passport needs to be returned for cancellation immediately and accompanied by a death certificate.
- Firearm Registration - Forward notarized copy of the Will and death certificate, registration number of the firearm(s), the seller licence, and buyer's licence number.

6.3 CREATING A WILL

It is advised to keep loved ones informed about your Will regularly to ensure there is complete understanding of your decisions, and also to manage the expectations of each family member, which will hopefully reduce later conflict. The right people must know where your recorded final affair information is.

It is important to note that only the original signed Will is valid. Copies of a Will are not accepted by the court. If only copies are found then the deceased is considered intestate. Please indicate on Will copies the location of the original Will.

Read the section on Estate Administration before creating your Will. Identify areas that may be of concern while making your own Will. Write down your concerns and discuss them with the proper professional help, ideally an estate lawyer.

WHY SHOULD I HAVE A WILL?

A Will ensures that your property is distributed the way you want. Some reasons why it is beneficial:

- You can choose your Executor(s).
- You can decide how your estate is to be distributed.
- You can choose who will take care of minor children or adult dependants.
- You may avoid a lengthy probate process.
- Estate administration is easier, faster, and less expensive.
- It minimizes estate taxes.
- You can make gifts and donations.
- It may avoid greater legal challenges.

If you have a Will, you can authorize an Executor to:

- Make choices to maximize tax benefits.
- Make choices about investments that would not otherwise be permitted.
- Create trust funds.
- Borrow money.
- Trade in assets.

WHO CAN MAKE A WILL?

The following are the qualifications an individual must have to create a Will:

- Must be 18 years of age.
- Must be mentally competent.
- Must understand the value and extent of your property and that it will be left to the named beneficiaries.

WHAT ARE THE REQUIREMENTS FOR SIGNING A FORMAL WILL?

For a Will to be valid, it must be:

- Completed in writing.
- Signed with two witnesses. The witness cannot be a beneficiary or the spouse/partner of a beneficiary.
- Free from force, threat, or undue influence by another party.

WHAT IS A HOLOGRAPHIC WILL?

A Holographic Will is a Will that is created entirely in the testator's own handwriting and signed by a testator. These Wills cannot be typed, and they do not need to be witnessed. While Holographic Wills are valid in some Canadian provinces, they are not recommended. It is important to note that issues most likely will arise when the Holographic Will is submitted for probate.

WHAT SHOULD BE INCLUDED IN A WILL?

In addition to the requirements for signing a formal Will, a Will also should include:

- Your legal name.
- An Executor.
- Legal guardians (if required).

If your estate will not be passing to one sole Executor and will be divided among more than one person, or you wish to designate specific items, then include:

- Real Property distribution (beneficiaries).

- Financial Asset distribution (beneficiaries).

- Personal Possession distribution (beneficiaries).

WHAT IS NOT INCLUDED IN A WILL?

Some assets do not have to be mentioned within a Will. These assets are called property outside a Will or estate. Please discuss with an estate lawyer to ensure proper distribution.

PROPERTY OUTSIDE OF WILL/ESTATE

*Please refer to the diagram, "What Makes Up Your Estate", on the next page.

Assets that have beneficiary designations completed upon creation are property outside of a Will/ estate. An Executor is not responsible for dealing with this property, no estate fees are attached, and these assets do not require probate; however, a documented list of all property outside a Will/ Estate is required by the courts for the probate process. Include a brief description and estimated value of the property, along with names of the joint owners and/or beneficiaries.

The transfer of property outside a Will/Estate occurs through the operation of law. These include assets with:

Right of Survivorship: Jointly owned bank accounts, land, property, or other assets registered in joint names with right of survivorship. Upon filing the necessary documents, the surviving joint owner becomes the asset's registered owner(s).

Policies with Named Beneficiaries: These assets may be passed directly to a named beneficiary without forming part of the estate. They can also be referred to as Property outside a Will/or Estate. Beneficiary designations of these properties are completed upon their establishment. For example:

- Life insurance policies.

- RRSPs or RRIFs payable to a named beneficiary.

What Makes Up Your Estate

Property Outside Will/Estate

Jointly Owned Assets
(Right of Survivorship)

- House
- Land/Property
- Vacation Property
- Bank Accounts (joint only)
- Etc.

Directly to Joint Owner
<u>NOT</u> PART OF WILL/ESTATE

Named Beneficiary
(Right of Survivorship)

Beneficiary named upon creation

- RRSP
- TFSA
- RESP
- RIFF
- Insurances (Life, Accidental, etc.)
- Investments with beneficiary
- Etc.

Directly to Named Beneficiary
<u>NOT</u> PART OF WILL/ESTATE

Your Estate

Estate
All Other Assets

- Digital Assets
- Land/Property
- Vacation Property
- Bank Accounts (not joint)
- Investments with no beneficiary
- Personal Property
- Etc.

Distributed through the Will

WHAT SHOULD I KNOW BEFORE I MAKE BEQUEATHS? ARE THERE LIMITATIONS ON DEALING WITH MY PROPERTY?

There are some situations where special considerations are required. As well, there are certain appointments and designations, where applicable, that must be included within your Will. To be sure that you understand these limitations, please seek the advice of an estate lawyer.

Minor Children

1. Minor children require a legal guardian in the situations below. Be aware, however, that legal guardianship may be challenged in court based on the child's best interest.

   - When minor children are children under the age of eighteen.

   - In the event of your death with no surviving parent.

   - If there is a legal agreement or court order that authorizes an appointment of a legal guardianship.

2. **Naming a Property Guardian for your minor children.**

   A Property Guardian is someone who will manage your children's property that passes through the estate.

   - Property Guardians can be Executors.

   - If a Property Guardian is required, but not identified, the court can appoint one.

   - A Property Guardian can also manage property not part of the estate (RRSP, etc.).

3. **Naming a trustee for beneficiaries who are minors.**

   An adult or a trustee is named the beneficiary to oversee the money in the minor's name until they are of age. In most cases the trustee is the legal guardian; however, it can be a separate individual.

Joint Property Limitations

Joint property is property owned by two or more people. Some examples are bank accounts, property, and land and includes the right of survivorship. Generally, jointly owned property does not form part of the deceased person's estate. Please verify with an estate lawyer before placing joint property in a Will.

Spouse's Rights and Family Property Limitations

Spouses are entitled to one-half of the combined family property, recognizing that both spouses contribute to childcare, household management, and financial support.

Married spouses may apply to the court to have the family property divided before the estate is managed under the Family Property Act. This includes couples who have lived together as spouses for two or more years.

Dependant's Rights

The law protects a dependant, such as your spouse, child or adult dependants, if you have inadequately provided for them. A dependant may include:

- Spouse by marriage.
- Someone you lived with as a spouse for at least two years.
- Someone you lived with for less than two years but have a child with.
- A child under the age of eighteen.
- A child over the age of eighteen who is mentally or physically unable to earn a living.
- Someone who ought to receive a more significant share of your estate because of need or other circumstances.
- Dependants must apply for relief within six months after Letters Probate or Letters of Administration are issued by the court.

Contractual Obligations

There are times when an estate may be bound to a contract previously entered by the deceased. Some examples would include child support, alimony, garnishees, or other court orders, leases, or mortgages, etc.

Tax Planning

Tax Planning is one of area that is often overlooked when making a Will, but it can have a major negative impact on the beneficiary if overlooked. Be sure you understand capital gains and other tax scenarios. Consult a tax accountant to understand the following before creating a Will:

- "Rollover" property to avoid capital gains tax on the estate.
- "Rollover" RRSPs to a spouse or dependant children.
- Defer or minimize taxes.
- Passing farm properties to the next generation.
- Passing business shares to other family members.

WHAT ABOUT DO-IT-YOURSELF WILL KITS?

Do-It-Yourself Will Kits are legal in Canada and some people feel that these kits are far more economical than creating a Will with an estate lawyer. While this may be true in the onset, a Will Kit may end up costing your estate much more in the long run.

If you decide to create a Will with a Will Kit, be aware of the following:

- Most Will Kits must go through probate and have a higher chance for litigation.

- The Will Kit wording may be too vague or too general. This can lead to disputes over interpretation, causing litigation.

- The Will Kit may not recognize provincial law or use the proper legal terminology or requirements. Keep in mind provincial law varies between provinces. Ensure your Will Kit includes the correct legal language and requirements according to your provincial law. Failure to do so can result in the Will being declared invalid by the courts, resulting in intestate.

- Will Kits do not prepare for specifics. Every estate is unique; each with its own set of situations, assets, liabilities and beneficiaries. It may be challenging to address your individual needs with a Will Kit. This may cause grounds for litigation.

If you have already created a Will with a Will Kit, it is best to have it reviewed by an estate lawyer to confirm that all requirements have been met.

After all is said and done, while it may cost you more to have a Will created with an estate lawyer, it will save your estate money in the end by eliminating or reducing the extensive court costs for intestate, probate, and litigation.

HOW DO I CANCEL MY WILL?

You can cancel a Will at any time by doing the following:

- Physically destroy it.
- Write or sign something with two witnesses stating you are changing or canceling your old Will.
- Make a new Will.

HOW DO I MAKE CHANGES TO MY WILL?

Changes to your Will can be made in the following ways:

- Minor changes can be made through an amendment or a codicil, which are separate legal documents created in addition to your Will.

- Changes can be made directly to your Will. If the changes are written by you in your own handwriting and signed by you, no witnesses are required. If it is not in your own handwriting, you and two witnesses must sign changes.

HOW DOES MARRIAGE OR COMMON LAW AFFECT WILLS?

- Any Will created before being married or living in a common law relationship for more than two years becomes invalid. For common law unions please refer to provincial law.

- Ending a spousal or common law relationship may also revoke a Will or some parts of it.

WHERE SHOULD I KEEP MY WILL FOR SAFEKEEPING?

A Will should be kept where the Executor can quickly locate it after the testator's death. **If the Executor does not have the original Will, they must know where to find it.** Again, only the original signed Will (not a copy) will be accepted by the courts.

Some examples of places to store your Will would be:

- A lawyer's office.
- A Court House (for a one-time fee, typically below $100.00).
- With your final affairs documentation.
- In a safe - ensure your Executor has the combination.
- Safety Deposit Box - However, be cautious of keeping your original Will in a safety deposit box and talk to your bank about access restrictions after death. Your Executor will require a copy of the Will to gain access, otherwise permission to access the safety deposit box must be granted by the courts.

HOW OFTEN SHOULD I REVIEW MY WILL?

Ideally, your Will should be reviewed at least once every three to five years or when the following situations apply:

- When property enters or exits your estate.
- When people enter or exit your life.
- When a relationship starts or ends.
- Upon the death of a beneficiary.
- When your children reach the age of eighteen.

- If you suddenly have an ill or disabled dependant requiring long-term financial support, even into adulthood.

- When children enter or leave spousal relationships, including step-children and grandchildren.

- When financial circumstances change.

WHAT IS A CODICIL?

Minor changes to a Will can be made through a codicil, a separate document created in addition to your Will. This addendum is written by you in your own handwriting and signed by you; no witnesses are required. However, if it is not in your own handwriting, you and two witnesses must sign changes.

Codicils should be done with an estate lawyer to reduce the chance of litigation. However, depending on the estate size, the cost of a codicil may be only slightly lower than the cost of redoing a Will.

WHAT ARE LETTERS OF INTENT?

A Letter of Intent, also called a Letter of Directive, is a document declaring the commitment of one party to do business with another. In the case of final affairs, the purpose would be to list specific items you want to give to individuals outside of your Will, usually smaller household items not typically included within a Will.

A sample Letter of Intent is included in Section 6.3 on page 223 of the worksheets. Items that may be included in a Letter of Intent are:

- Smaller items of sentimental value.

- Specific items (household or small property such as furniture, jewelry, china, artwork, knick-knacks, etc.) that you want to give to certain individuals.

Think about minor things such as clothing, kitchenware, furniture, etc. that must go somewhere. Look at distribution between friends, relatives, and charities.

Have valuable items appraised with the appraisal sent to the recipient for adequate insurance.

At times, distributing such items may become challenging and may cause friction. Talk with your Executor to make your wishes clear and trust your Executor to distribute your possessions in the way you intend. If you are particular about certain items, put them in your Will.

Ensure your good intentions are received. It is strongly suggested you talk with your family and gift recipients. Be sure they understand your wishes and are willing and able to receive them.

Another option is to gift these items before death, to experience and share the joy of giving during your lifetime.

WHY SHOULD I USE AN ESTATE LAWYER?

There are many types of lawyers who specialize in many areas. There are real estate lawyers, criminal justice lawyers, family law lawyers, the list goes on. Each are specifically trained and have experience in their areas of expertise. The same applies to estate lawyers.

The estate lawyer:

- Ensures a Will is legal and valid.

- Reduces the risk of litigation.

- Is trained to watch out for any areas of concern.

- Has the knowledge, expertise and experience in the field of estate law.

- Is there to protect you.

If you live in a location where there is limited choices for legal representation, for example some small towns only have one lawyer, please keep in mind the following:

- If your estate is large, complex or has challenging situations, it may be in your best interest to seek the advice of an experienced estate lawyer in another location.

- Lawyers are people too! They retire, move, become sick and can suddenly pass away. If you use a lawyer from a rural location or one with a small practice, understand what will happen to your files, legal history and documents when your lawyer no longer practices.

6.4 Checklists for Survivors and Executors

The following checklists are for both a surviving spouse and your Executors. There may be other required duties, depending on the estate and provincial laws. Be sure to enlist the assistance of an estate lawyer or trustee.

SURVIVOR'S CHECKLIST

- Notify friends and family.

- Deal with intentions as to donation of organs.

- Locate the Will and pass it onto the Executor.

- Determine if there are specific instructions for funeral services in the Will that you will need to establish with the Executor.

- If there is no Will or it cannot be found, you may need to apply for Letters of Administration through court.

- Work with the Executor to provide information and locate critical documentation required to complete the Checklist for Executor.

- Cancel any planned trips.

- Stack and store any incoming mail.

- Call your employer and your spouse's employer for information about relevant benefits.

- Apply for death benefits and survivor benefits; applications are available through funeral homes or the government websites.

- Contact where applicable:
    - o   Child Tax Credit
    - o   GST
    - o   Provincial Pension Plan

- Beware of creditor claims. A legitimate debt of your spouse is not your debt unless you have signed for it, or your late spouse incurred it to provide for him or herself with necessities. They could be fraudulent, as some con artists pick their victims through the obituaries. If the debt is unsecured, decide for yourself if you wish to pay for it. Do not be pressured to pay any such debt quickly. If uncertain, seek legal advice.

- Probate might not be necessary if you and your spouse held everything jointly. For example, if you are the beneficiary of all life insurance, RRSPs and RRIFs, and if you are the Executor. Please secure the advice of an estate lawyer for appropriate information.

- Hold life insurance proceeds or other cash amounts in highly secure, highly liquid investments such as a bank savings account or a money market mutual fund. Do not rush into any long-term investments or financial commitments.

EXECUTOR CHECKLIST

Immediate:

- If there are children under the age of eighteen, or if there are dependant adults, notify the Public Guardian and Trustee.

- Notify friends and family.

- Deal with intentions as to donation of organs.

- Arrange for care/adoption of any pets.

- Locate the Will, any codicils, or memoranda.

- Locate and review all completed final affair documentation.

- Review the Will to determine if there are any special instructions for the funeral. Assist with the arrangements. The Executor signs off on funeral arrangements.

- Obtain a death certificate. In Canada, secure the Funeral Director's Statement of Death or apply for a Provincial Death Certificate (required for land title registry and insurance companies).

- Publish an obituary.

- Publish an advertisement for creditors and others before distributing assets to protect from liability.

- Pay funeral bills. Arrange for the funeral service to be paid through the deceased's financial institution.

- Establish immediate cash requirements for the family.

- Hire an estate lawyer.

- Verify that proper insurance is in place to protect all real assets, homes, vehicles, vacation properties, etc.

Within the First Month:

- Terminate a lease or arrange to sublet if the deceased lived in a rental property.

- Open an estate bank account.

- Transfer balances of existing bank accounts to the estate bank account. In the case of joint accounts, with the right of survivorship, provide the financial institution with death certificates and request transfer of the funds to the surviving joint tenant.

- Re-direct or cancel any pre-authorized electronic debits or credits to the estate account.

- Cancel credit cards and confirm outstanding balances.

- File claims for life insurance, including any group insurance policies.

- If applicable, apply for pension plan death benefits, survivor's benefits, orphan's benefits, and other death benefits. A copy of the death certificate will be required.

- Notify the various agencies and organizations that must be contacted upon death. See "Contacts: Other" Worksheet on page 131. Please note that some places may require a death certificate.

- Cancel health insurance coverage.

- Cancel or complete outstanding broker's orders.

- Cancel driver's licence.

- Cancel utilities, including cable, internet, telephone, and cell phone. Request refunds where applicable.

- Cancel memberships.

- Contact the post office to re-route mail.

- Cancel any house cleaning or yard care contracts.

- Return the deceased's passport to the government passport office or any other country for which the deceased has a passport.

- Cancel magazine, newspaper or other subscriptions.

- Fill out declarations of transmission and Powers of Attorney required to transfer securities.

- Keep extensive records of all assets coming in and going out of the estate.

- Keep documentation on the reasoning behind all decisions made regarding the estate.

Within the First Six Months:

- List the beneficiaries and their addresses. Notify them of the benefits to be received under the Will.

- Meet with an estate lawyer to complete the applications for probate of the estate. Arrange payment for any applicable fees.

- Obtain appropriate court orders, letters probate or letters of administration.

- Call in the estate. Inventory the assets and liabilities. Locate the deceased's assets and liabilities and determine their value. List their value and full particulars, including certificate number, registration particulars, maturity dates, interest rates, payment, and frequency dates. Write to financial institutions, employers, insurance companies, brokers, and RRSP/PRRIF trustees.

- Obtain titled documents for real property, mortgages, share certificates, debentures, bonds, and guaranteed investment certificates.

- Arrange for valuations of all major assets such as real estate, personal property, securities, and vehicles.

- Access and list the contents of safety deposit boxes.

- Transfer title for all real property to the estate.

- Check banking records for any unclaimed account balances of the deceased.

- Review the investment portfolio.

- Notify bond and dividend disbursing agents to change the address of record.

- Review the Will to determine the plan of asset distribution. Consult with the beneficiaries regarding specific distribution (distribution in-kind) where appropriate.

- Review with the estate lawyer any time frames or restrictions on distribution of the estate. For example, any family law situations or dependant's relief applications.

Complete Estate Administration:

- Terminate safety deposit boxes.

- Arrange for the sale of securities if they are being converted to cash or arrange for transfer of securities and re-register if required.

- Deliver personal effects and obtain receipts. Plan for the safe custody of personal valuables of the deceased.

- Arrange for sale or distribution of assets not specifically left to a beneficiary. Obtain sufficient notarial copies for the transfer of assets once probate is granted. Place all money from the sale of assets into an estate bank account.

- If the Will provides outright distribution, obtain a release for distribution, and transfer assets or funds to beneficiaries. Maintain enough funds in reserve for income taxes and any outstanding accounts.

- If a Will provides for trusts, set up testamentary trusts and arrange for ongoing review of the investments and continuous compliance within the rest of the terms of the trust.

- Prepare and file proper government trust information return forms.

- Obtain provincial and federal tax clearance.

- Regularly report on the progress of administration of the estate to beneficiaries. Provide each beneficiary with a copy of the inventory of assets and liabilities.

- Prepare for payment of legacies and interim distributions. Deliver gifts and obtain receipts.

- Deliver securities. Obtain receipts if distribution in kind.

- Arrange for any rollover or transfer of registered investment proceeds, such as RRSPs.

- Arrange for the passing of accounts, if there are disputes amongst the beneficiaries. (This is asking the court to approve your estate's financial records and your plan for the distribution of the estate).

- Invest surplus cash following the terms of the Will.

- Pay bills and finalize the debts of the deceased and the estate. Settle all debts and claims.

- Calculate Executor's compensation.

- Request estate lawyer's bill.

- Prepare accounts for passing or approval of beneficiaries. Ask the estate lawyer to prepare releases. Disclose accounting to all beneficiaries and request approval. Have each adult beneficiary approve this accounting by signing a release.

- Distribute the estate according to the Will.

- Obtain releases from beneficiaries required to complete the distribution of the estate.

- If accounts are challenged and to be audited by the court, ask the estate lawyer to prepare the application and all required notices and arrange an appointment.

- Distribute any remaining funds or deliver assets.

In Canada:

- Locate tax returns from the prior year. Prepare and file within six months of the date of death any T1 returns for the previous years. T4-ACP, as well as an OAS Statement, must be requested from Service Canada if applicable. Complete Income Tax Returns and obtain the Income Tax Clearance Certificate required to complete the estate distribution.

- Prepare and file necessary tax returns for foreign assets, if any.

- Prepare and file Terminal T1 Tax Return and other returns with Revenue Canada. Request a Clearance Certificate.

- With the FINAL Tax Return, you must include a copy of the death certificate, the Will, and Letters Probate. Get a copy of the **GUIDE FOR PREPARING T1 RETURNS FOR DECEASED PERSONS**. Contact Canada Customs and Revenue Agency. You will require the deceased's Social Insurance Number.

6.5 ESTATE ADMINISTRATION

WHAT DOES DISTRIBUTING THE ESTATE MEAN?

The estate's administrator or Executor is responsible for distributing the decedent's property as it is bequeathed in the Last Will and Testament.

- Executors/Administrators must wait for 6 months after Letters Probate or Letters of Administration to distribute the estate to allow for dependants and spouses to apply for relief.

- Executors may obtain written permission from dependants or spouses who consent to an earlier distribution.

- Executors must obtain a final CRA Tax Clearance prior to final estate distribution.

- Executors must present a final statement of accounts to beneficiaries for approval.

- Executors must obtain a legal release form from each beneficiary stating that the beneficiary has received their gift and release the Executor from further legal repercussions.

WHO DISTRIBUTES AN ESTATE?

- If the deceased has left a Will and named an Executor, the Executor will conduct the estate administration.

- If the deceased does not name an Executor or does not have a Will, their next of kin or another interested party may apply for Letters of Administration with the court.

HOW LONG DOES IT TAKE TO SETTLE AN ESTATE?

Settling an estate takes around 18 months or more, depending on the size of the estate or the complexity. Again, some other factors that can prolong settling an estate are business holdings, challenging family or beneficiaries, the estate size, or difficulties with an Executor.

WHAT HAPPENS FIRST WHEN SOMEONE DIES?

Attend to Urgent Matters

- Attend to the immediate needs of the bereaved.

- Are there dependants or pets to arrange care for?

- Who must be immediately notified?

- Are there organ or tissue donations?

- Is an autopsy required?

- Are there religious or spiritual observances?

- If the deceased died away from home, arrangements must be made to return the deceased to his or her city or town.

- Secure any physical assets of the deceased. Are windows closed and doors locked within their home? Do they have a vehicle somewhere where it may be towed?

- As soon as possible, locate the Will. Not only does the Will state who is to be Executor, but it may also contain funeral direction.

Finding the Will

- Locate the Will. Determine if there may be other Wills in existence by speaking with a spouse or past lawyers. Many Wills are stored at the local courthouse. Search Wills and Estates Registry.

- If it is believed a person is holding a Will, an Executor can serve notice for that person to appear in court. The individual then must provide any information they have regarding the location of the Will.

- Before declaring intestate, there must be a proven, extensive search for a Will.

Reading the Will

- After recovering the Will, determine if there are any funeral instructions.

- Determine the Executor(s) and notify them immediately. Ensure they have the original Will and not a copy.

- A formal reading of the Will with beneficiaries present is no longer required; however, each beneficiary must be notified in writing. An estate lawyer can instruct you on the legal requirements for this step.

- Obtain the services of an estate lawyer for the estate. The lawyer will provide the Executor guidance on Will interpretation, outline Executor responsibilities and legal obligations. The estate lawyer will discuss estate distribution timelines, litigation issues and answer any questions the Executor may have.

WHAT HAPPENS WHEN THERE IS NO WILL (INTESTATE)?

Intestate is when an individual dies without a Will, which can result in challenging situations.

- It may be hard to trace relatives who may be entitled to inherit.

- It may be difficult to locate all property and belongings.

- It must be proven to the courts that an extensive, documented search for the original Will has been conducted, without success.

- In some Canadian provinces, property is divided according to the Intestate Succession Act, which is a hierarchy of a series of relatives predetermined by the provincial courts.

WHAT IS ESTATE MANAGEMENT?

This is performing all duties of the Executor from time of death until the estate is closed. The Executor has many responsibilities during this time including fiduciary and legal responsibilities. It is common to feel overwhelmed, confused and frustrated. There is professional help available for the Executor. Many trust companies or other financial institutions offer Executor assistance. Executors can also enlist the services of a Certified Executor Advisor.

Below are some duties of managing an estate. For a more detailed list, please see "Executor Checklist" on page 65.

- Apply for probate.

- When necessary, obtain all documentation managed by the Power of Attorney.

- Secure and manage all physical assets of the estate. Ensure they are protected from physical damage (such as deterioration from the elements and theft) or from any liability issues.

- Create an inventory of major assets and liabilities.

- Contact any organization or agency that will require notification upon death.

- Manage accounting, finances, and trust (if required) of the estate.

- Keep extremely detailed documentation for any decisions made regarding the estate. These details may be necessary if there is litigation action.

- Identify any death benefits or insurances.

- Obtain appraisal valuations if required.

- Where necessary, liquidate assets.

- Once administration is complete, the Executor must complete a proposed distribution.

WHAT ARE LETTERS PROBATE?

Letters Probate is a court order that formally recognizes that a Will is valid and that an Executor is entitled to manage the estate.

Special circumstances for probate exist when an estate is small. For example, if there is real property and the total value of the estate is under $15 000.00, or there is no real property and the full value of the estate is under $25 000.00.

An Executor must probate the will within 60 days of the date of death. If the Executor does not meet this deadline, they can be summoned to appear in court to produce the Will.

DO I NEED TO PROBATE?

Requiring probate depends on the type of assets owned by the deceased and how ownership of those assets is registered.

In many cases, probate is required before distributing the deceased's property, including but not limited to, real property, agencies, banks, insurance companies, etc. The Will must go through probate if there are any land title transfers. It may also be required by institutions holding property of the deceased.

Typically, a Letters Probate package is available online. The courts require several documents before granting Letters Probate. These documents must be signed by a Commissioner for Oaths. The documents include:

- **Affidavit of Execution of Will** with the original Will attached. A witness to the Will must swear in an affidavit stating that they witnessed the testator's signature. This is typically completed at the time a Will is created with a lawyer.

- **Application for Grant of Probate**: This includes information about the deceased and beneficiaries. It will include the date of death and a request for probate.

- **Affidavit of Executor**: A sworn document by the Executor that requests probate and contains the promise of the Executor to properly administer the estate.

- **Statement of Property**: A document that outlines all known assets of the deceased, with their value to be administered by the Executor. It also includes a statement with a description and the estimated value of the property outside a Will that does NOT form part of the estate, such as joint property, life insurances, RRSPs, etc.

- **If applicable, a certificate** that there is no one under the age of eighteen with interest in the estate.

WHAT ARE LETTERS OF ADMINISTRATION?

When an Executor is not named in a Will, the courts determine an estate administrator to distribute the estate. Interested parties may apply to the court for authorization to act as administrators of the estate. By law, there is a priority for who can apply:

- Individuals who apply must have the approval of other interested parties who have greater or equal rights to apply.

- Up to three people may jointly apply.

- In addition to the Letters Probate document, administrators must also include:
    - **Letters of Administration**
    - **Letters of Administration with Will Annexed** (A Will exists but with no named Executor, or Executor is unable or unwilling to act.)

CAN A PERSON REFUSE TO ACT AS AN EXECUTOR?

Yes. A person must fill out a Renunciation of Probate form indicating they are giving up the appointment as Executor. This will allow an alternate named Executor to apply for Letters Probate or another person to apply for Letters of Administration.

CAN YOU REPLACE AN EXECUTOR?

- An Executor can be replaced if the current Executor cannot serve or no longer wishes to serve.

- If an Executor is not fulfilling their duties, an application can be made to have them removed.

- An interested person may seek legal counsel and apply to the courts to review the estate accounts if they feel the Executor's actions are illegal, negligent or not acting in the best interest of the estate.

- If the Will does not include an Alternate Executor, another person will have to apply to the courts to become the successor.

- When possible, the previous Executor must pass the accounts formally to the new Executor. This must be completed within two years of the Letters Probate grant.

- If the beneficiaries sign a release, the Executor can ask the court to discharge them without passing the accounts.

WHAT IS THE DEPENDANT'S RELIEF ACT?

The Dependant's Relief Act ensures that any legal dependant of the deceased is entitled to reasonable provision for their maintenance. It allows dependants, or a legal representative for the dependant, to make a claim to the courts if they have not been adequately provided for within the deceased's Will. A dependant includes the deceased spouse, common law spouse, minor children and any adult child dependants. An adult child dependant is a person who is over the age of 18 and who is mentally or physically unable to earn a living and is financially dependant upon the deceased.

WHAT IS THE FAMILY PROPERTY ACT?

The Family Property Act establishes how family property is viewed in some provinces in Canada. This law observes that both spouses contribute to childcare, household management, and financial support. It states that each spouse is typically entitled to an equal share of their family property. If the spouse is not named within the Will, then there is a six month time limit from date of probate for a spouse to make a claim on the estate. If you are in a common law relationship, please review your rights under provincial law.

WHAT IS A PUBLIC GUARDIAN AND TRUSTEE?

A Public Guardian and Trustee is an appointed representative for children under eighteen or any dependant adults who have an interest or a claim in an estate. This position is appointed by the courts if no one else represents the dependant. The Public Guardian and Trustee is there to ensure a dependant's property interests are protected. Their tasks would include:

- Overseeing the estate and investment accounting on behalf of the dependant.
- Provide any consent necessary for any dealing with an estate.

DO I HAVE TO NOTIFY THE CANADA REVENUE AGENCY?

Once an Executor has filed all the necessary tax returns, paid all amounts owing, and received all related Notices of Assessment, a Clearance Certificate may be requested from the Canada Revenue Agency. A Clearance Certificate indicates that the deceased person has no outstanding tax liabilities with the CRA.

WHAT ARE CREDITORS?

Creditors are any person or entity with a financial claim against the deceased. These claims are estate debts, which are the debts owed by the deceased at the date of death. The Executor must identify the estate's debts and pay all estate obligations before distributing them to beneficiaries. To do this, they must:

- Review the deceased's personal papers and make inquiries to determine any owed debts.
- Conduct a personal property lien search and a judgment registry search.

- Complete a Notice to Creditors form provided by the court to be advertised for two weeks. It must include a deadline for any creditor to notify the Executor.

WHEN IS THE ESTATE INSOLVENT?

An estate is considered insolvent when there are insufficient assets to pay all estate debts.

- Funeral and administration expenses are paid before other creditors.
- Priority for debt payment is established through the Administration of Estates Act.

WHAT ARE SOME OF THE COSTS RELATED TO ESTATE ADMINISTRATION?

Probate Tax: A tax imposed on the probate of every Will and/or grant of every estate that surpasses a predetermined dollar value. This is a set fee, similar to the fee charged within a real estate transaction. Probate fees differ between provinces. At the time of print, probate fees are approximately $7.00 for every $1,000.00 of estate assets. Please contact an estate lawyer to determine exact probate fees.

Rules of Court Costs: Court costs are set out in the Fees Regulations. These apply only to the value of the assets solely owned by the deceased and form part of the estate. It does not apply to assets outside the estate or jointly owned assets. These are paid to the court when applying for Letters Probate or Letters of Administration.

Payments to the Public Guardian and Trustee: The Public Guardian and Trustee may have costs fixed or ordered taxed by the court. The court shall specify from what source or by what party the costs of the Public Guardian and Trustee are to be paid.

Legal Fees: These are fees for the lawyer representing the Executor and are set out in the Rules of Court. These are core services directly related to estate administration and are based on a percentage of the estate value. They include:

- Tariff amount: These are set fees that lawyers are allowed to charge based on the value of an estate.
- Meeting with the Executor.
- Reviewing the Will.
- Gathering information about the deceased's property and debts.
- Distributing assets of the estate.

Non-core services include:

- Locating beneficiaries.
- Obtaining bonds.
- Paying bills and dealing with creditors.
- Distributing personal belongings.
- Dealing with joint tenancy issues.
- Dealing with life insurance policies, pensions, and investments not payable to the estate.
- Dealing with tax returns and clearance certificates.
- Matters related to the passing of accounts.

Land Transfer Costs: These are fees for when land title is transferred to the estate and then again to the beneficiaries. If applicable, there is also a fee to obtain the Public Guardian and Trustee's consent to sell land left to a child.

Executor or Estate Administrator Fees: Executors and administrators have a right to be paid reasonable compensation according to the difficulty of the estate and the amount of work handled. Discuss these fees with a lawyer. Please read "Does an Executor Get Paid?" under *Choosing an Executor* on page 52 in this chapter for further information.

WHAT ARE COMMON PROBLEMS IN ESTATE ADMINISTRATION?

Executors are encouraged to seek legal advice to assist with problems that arise. At times, Wills are disputed. If the matter cannot be resolved between the parties, the court can assign a mediator or make an order that settles the issue. Most legal fees can be charged to the estate.

WHAT ARE THE MAIN GROUNDS FOR CHALLENGING A WILL?

Dependant Disputes

Some specific responsibilities and obligations are required for particular beneficiaries. Also, there are limitations on a Will. Contesting a Will on these grounds can look like the following:

- Dependants have not been adequately provided for in a Will.
- A spouse is entitled to half of the family property.

- It is considered a moral obligation to make provisions for all dependants. Wills may be challenged if there are no provisions made for dependants or a dependant's spouse. Failure to provide may result in a court order varying the Will in the dependant's favor.
- Disputes arise concerning child custody.

Validity of Will

If there is doubt that a Will is valid or does not meet the legal requirements, a request to the court can be made. Evidence from witnesses involved in Will preparation or medical experts will determine if:

- The Will was improperly signed or witnessed.
- It is believed that the Will-maker did not have full knowledge of or approve the signed Will.
- It is believed that the Will was forged or was replaced by a fraudulent one.
- The Will was not properly created. Validity can be questioned if it was not done in writing, not signed in the presence of two witnesses, or the signer was not of legal age.
- The deceased lacked the mental capacity to make the Will (incapacity). For example, they had dementia or other medical conditions that affected their judgment.
- The deceased was pressured or under duress while making the Will. Undue influence means the Will-maker created the Will under force, fear, or in a manner that overbeared or coerced the Will-maker to change their Will.

Common Issues

- Beneficiaries feel the Executor's compensation or other fees are too high or not appropriate.
- Disputes over inheritances.
- Disputes arise over the sale of property or personal assets.
- The testator was not aware of all the property they owned or disposed of.
- Outstanding liabilities or claims against the estate, an Executor or trustee.
- Someone refusing to turnover assets belonging to the estate.
- Disputes over guardianship or committees of the estate.
- Trusts are contested.
- Mishandling of estate management.
- Disputes over the estate's records.

SUMMARY

Congratulations! You made it through the chapter! Please keep in mind this chapter's highlights:

Create a Legal Will

A Will may be the most crucial document that you ever write. Don't risk leaving behind a big mess for your family and friends. Create a Will and be assured that you are taking care of the people you love.

Estate Lawyer

To avoid litigation, be sure the Will is created legally and accurately. For this reason, it is strongly recommended that you make your Will with an estate lawyer.

Keep the Will Up to Date

Life changes. It is best to revisit your Will periodically or upon major life events. Reviewing this document helps to ensure that your Will still reflects your wishes.

Choose Your Executor Wisely

It is natural to gravitate toward family or close friends when choosing an Executor. This is a time to decide with your head and not your heart.

Choosing the right Executor can prevent costly issues. Ensure your Executor has the skills and time needed to perform the required duties and tasks. Be certain your Executor is fully aware of this responsibility and is willing to accept this role.

Discuss Your Will with Your Family

While there is no magic that makes these conversations easy, if you keep in mind the important things, you can move toward successful communication. All your careful planning will be wasted if your beneficiaries feud and contest your Will. Conversations eliminate any elements of surprise, reduce the risk of disagreements, and give you a chance to provide clarity about what you are doing. They will help your family understand why you think your plans are the best course of action.

Location, Location, Location

Finally, even the best Will won't be effective if no one knows where to find it. Ensure your family and your Executor know where your Will is kept.

Section 7
FUNERAL/MEMORIAL ARRANGEMENTS

This may be the most difficult section for people to plan. No one wants to think about their own death and planning a final service ahead of time seems so...final; however, there are many good reasons to pre-plan your funeral services.

The reality is your loved ones will be in a state of grief, which is not the best time for making decisions. Pre-planning allows your loved ones to be with those who can provide comfort and support rather than dealing with the additional strain of making funeral arrangements.

Pre-planning your service can save you (and your estate) money. You can determine the cost of various services and products by shopping around. **Families often emotionally overspend by hundreds, even thousands, of dollars when purchasing funeral arrangements**. Overspending is common for several reasons:

- The emotional impact of losing someone can cloud judgment.

- There are often pressing time constraints.

- Many on-the-spot decisions must be made.

- Most families have no prior experience in funeral planning.

- People believe it is what their loved one wanted or deserved.

Pre-planning is sparing your loved ones from these situations. Where possible, include your loved ones in the planning process. This allows you to discuss your wishes with your loved ones ahead of time, and to ensure they know all important and necessary information.

*It is not recommended to put funeral instructions within the Will. Locating the Will can take time and it may not be located prior to a funeral.

BE SURE TO LIST:

- Funeral Home Name and Representative.

- Cemetery Contact Information.

- Funeral Funding Company or Insurance: If you have coverage, such as Purple Shield or a similar plan, this information should be placed in this section as well.

- Service wishes/plans.

- Burial plans.

No matter what you choose, be sure to have your wishes in writing and the person responsible for overseeing your funeral arrangements informed where this information is.

WHAT ARE THE COSTS ASSOCIATED WITH FUNERALS AND BURIALS?

Funeral and burial costs today can easily cost thousands of dollars. Prices vary between different funeral homes and cemeteries. Understand your options before purchasing anything or selecting a funeral home or cemetery.

With pre-planning your funeral and burial arrangements, you are able to reduce some of the stress and financial responsibilities on loved ones when you die. An increasing number of people are making advance plans to cover these costs. Funeral and burial costs are paid through the deceased's estate if they are not prepaid.

Many funeral homes charge a basic service or professional service fee, regardless of the arrangement. This service fee may include obtaining copies of the death certificate, securing any required permits, sheltering the remains, and coordinating the arrangements. This fee will not include the optional services or products offered. Also, be aware that sometimes cemetery costs are separate from funeral home costs; confirm these costs with your funeral home.

When researching understand the charges for the following:

- Basic service or professional service fees
- Viewing
- Burial
- Transportation of remains
- Casket/urn
- Embalming and other preparation
- Cemetery plot or columbarium site
- Monument, headstone, or marker

Some of the above may be optional. As well, depending on what type of service will be held, there are many other choices. Money can be saved with planning and by understanding the different services and the associated costs.

SHOULD I CREMATE?

Cremation is incinerating a body so that only ashes remain, whereas with a burial, the body remains intact. The decision to cremate or not is a personal choice, but you may wish to discuss the option of cremation with your family members, loved ones, or seek the counsel of your faith leader or a funeral professional.

Consider the following:

Different Options
In the case of a burial, the body can be interred in the ground or entombed in a mausoleum. By comparison, cremated remains can be kept by the family, scattered, buried in the ground, or entombed in a columbarium. Of the two, cremation is generally the more economical choice.

Different Cultures and Faiths
Your culture or your faith may have an impact on your decision. Religions and cultures have many various views on cremation, and they vary greatly. For some, cremation is a requirement while, for others, it is forbidden.

Environmental Impact

If being environmentally friendly is important to you, then there are some things to consider. Biodegradability of products and fluids, and possible air pollutants are just two of the things that may impact your decision. As well, the popularity of natural or eco-friendly (or green) options are also on the rise. Do your research or consult with a funeral professional to help with your choice, as there are both pros and cons to these options.

WHY SHOULD I HAVE A FUNERAL?

A funeral or a memorial service is an important need for those left behind to mourn. While it is fine if you don't wish to have a funeral, it is important for those you love to have some type of gathering or service for the following reasons:

- It allows people to acknowledge the passing of a loved one and to honour their life.

- It is for people to mourn together and provide support for each other.

- It is a reflection and remembrance of the loved one's life.

- It plays an important part in healthy healing after a loss. It helps with the transition and acceptance of loss.

- It provides meaning in loss and is a chance to show how a person mattered.

- It recognizes the impact that a person's life had on others.

WHAT SHOULD I CONSIDER WHEN PLANNING A SERVICE?

Today's life celebrations can take on many different names and many different forms. The choices are many. It is important to know that there is no right or wrong way. The following are a few things to consider when planning a service.

- **Coffin or Urn**: Determine the style and material you would like your coffin or urn to be made from. Decide if you are purchasing an urn from a funeral home, retailer, or artisan.

- **Type of Service**: Traditional religious ceremony, memorial, celebration-of-life, or other.

- **Location of service**: Church or other location. Consider the requirements for the size of service and reserved space for family members.

- **Length of service.**

- **Viewing of the body.**

- **Transportation of family.**

- **Processional and closing.**

- **Special activities during the service.**

- **Officiant:** Provide the funeral home with the name and contact information if there is a person selected to conduct a service.

- **Eulogy:** Provide the name and contact information of the person/people giving the eulogy.

- **Pallbearers:** Provide names and contact information for pallbearers.

- **Memorial cards:** Provide the name of the person who will be responsible for gathering the information required for memorial cards. Verify this person knows all details and where to locate the material. Consider doing this yourself ahead of time.

- **Music and special readings:** List your preferences and, if applicable, who will be reading or performing.

- **Flowers:** What types and colours of flowers would you prefer?

- **Photos/slide show:** Do you want a photo display or a slide presentation? What photos would you like? Consider who will be responsible for putting this together, as this can be a very time-consuming and emotional project. Have photos ready or indicate where photos can be located. Consider gathering photos ahead of time.

- **After service gathering:** Location of gathering needs to be determined.

- **Food:** If any food is required for an after service gathering, what kind of food is to be offered, and who will serve and prepare it?

- **Charitable donations:** Would you like to select a charitable organization to receive donations in your name?

- **Support people:** Who will be there to support a survivor?

WHAT SHOULD I KNOW ABOUT THE OBITUARY, EULOGY AND MEMORIAL CARDS?

While obituaries are not a requirement, many people create one out of tradition. **Do NOT assume your loved ones know all your information.** Make note of all the details you want mentioned in your obituary, eulogy, and on your memorial card, where applicable. You could even take this one step further and write your own, or with the assistance of someone else.

- Document your personal history. Put this data in one place or list where it can be found. Confirm that the person overseeing your funeral or memorial, as well as your Executor, knows where to find your history.

- Research cost and publication of obituaries. Consider size, the number of print days, and the city or town of publication. Many funeral homes will have publication costs. Keep in mind, the larger the obituary, and the more often it appears, the more expensive it will be.

- Know the cost of memorial cards.

- What photo would you like in your obituary? In your memorial card?

- Decide how to list family. (Blended family listings, correct name spelling, etc.)

- Name and address of service. Include the city of service if the obituary is to be published in multiple papers.

- If applicable, name and address for donations to any charity.

WHAT IF I CHOOSE TO NOT HAVE A BURIAL?

In some provinces, the burial of a human body requires a permit and a designated plot for interment. However, if you choose cremation, it is your personal choice what you would like done with the ashes.

Depending on local municipal or provincial regulations, cremated remains can be scattered over fields or water, kept in a house, deposited in private gardens, or interred in a cemetery or columbarium. Consult with the municipal authority before scattering cremated remains.

WHAT DO I NEED TO KNOW IF I AM HAVING A BURIAL?

- Interment (burial) vs. entombment (crypt, mausoleum, etc.)

- Decide if the committal will take place before or after the service, or on a different day. Depending on what part of the country you live in, you may wish your burial to take place in a different season.

- Burial place, funeral plots, crypts, etc.

- Headstones: style, material, epitaph.

- If burial is preferred, provide the details of the cemetery arrangements.

- If you have not purchased a burial plot, this may be the time to do so.

WHAT SHOULD I KNOW BEFORE CHOOSING A FUNERAL HOME?

Meeting with a funeral home representative to discuss your plans ahead of time is easier than before an event requiring immediate decisions. You should feel comfortable with your funeral director. Don't be afraid to ask questions. Chances are, no matter what you ask, they have answered it before, many times.

- Know if the funeral home you are considering is independently run or if it is owned by a corporation. What is their reputation like in the community?

- Some funeral homes are commission based, while others are not. Understand that this may mean you are being upsold. Typically, independent funeral homes do not run based on commissions.

- Ask if there are funeral packages available and what the cost difference is between those and customized services.

- Inquire about payment options.

- Shop around and compare costs. Understand your options and align those choices with your budget.

WHAT INFORMATION AND ITEMS ARE REQUIRED BY THE FUNERAL HOME?

Death Certificate Information

- Full legal name of the deceased.

- Social Insurance Number.

- Date of birth and place of birth. This information can be found on the birth certificate. If born at home, an address or land location may be required.

- Date of death.

- Location of death.

- Address at the time of death.

- Marital status, and if applicable, surviving spouse's name.

- Father's full name.

- Mother's full name, including maiden name.

Information for Funeral Home

- Name of Executor.

- Name of family contact for information and communication.

- Name of spouse/partner.

- Names of children and grandchildren.

- Names of parents.

- Names of any predeceased family members.

- List of accomplishments: highest level of education and occupation.

- List of any special thanks.

- Interment details.

- Memorial donations.

Items

- Recent photograph of the deceased.

- Clothing: This is required if you are planning a viewing or prefer special clothing for a cremation or a casket burial.

- Eyeglasses and jewelry: These items may remain with the deceased or be removed and returned to the family after the service.

SUMMARY

At no point should you feel pressured into making any arrangements that are unwanted or make you feel uncomfortable. To help you with your plans, talk with family and friends about any funerals that they have experienced. Ultimately, it does not matter what your final wishes are, but that you have left instructions for your family to follow when the time comes.

Section 8
IMPORTANT DOCUMENTATION

This section identifies important documents that require original hard copies for the various duties of a Power of Attorney and Executor. It also describes other material that might be of interest to your family. Examples for each are provided. Some of these items may be difficult to locate. Starting the search for these papers now allows you time to locate them.

DOCUMENTS

Death Certificates

There are different types of Death Certificates that will be required for different functions.

- Funeral Director Statement of Death: for banks and insurances (provided at time of arrangement).
- Provincial Death Certificate: for Land Titles (application process may take up to 5 weeks).
- Death certificates can be obtained by contacting your provincial government.

Passports

The passport will need to be cancelled immediately after death and must be accompanied by a Statement of Death.

Other Documents

These documents can be obtained by contacting provincial and local government, schools and religious institutions. Please include any other information you may feel is relevant here.

Social Insurance Card	Prenuptial agreement
Health Services Card	Co-habitation agreement
Birth Certificate	Child Custody and Support paper
Marriage Licence	Citizenship Card
Immunization Records	Change of Name Certificate
Divorce papers	Naturalization Certificate
Separation agreement	

SUMMARY

Having your documents in a centralized location is one of the most helpful things you can do for your partner, Power of Attorney, and Executor. It may not seem important, but it is vital to those who handle your affairs.

Section 9
FAMILY INFORMATION

This section is designed to help you provide your family history, which can be passed down from generation to generation. It is a place to gather memorabilia and for you to record written memories that a family can share. It is a wonderful gift to your loved ones!

Currently, genealogy is a trend. With today's technology, more people research their family histories to trace lineage, to determine genetic medical history, or simply do it out of curiosity. Any information you provide is a great help to future generations.

Please note: Particular family history is important for filling out certain forms. For example, death certificates require birth location. In the event of a home birth, an address or land location where the birth took place would be necessary.

This section is also a great place to leave letters to your loved ones after you are gone. Sometimes it is easier to write down feelings or thoughts in a way you have always meant to do, or it is a way to communicate with those dear to you when you can't. Creating final letters to your loved ones lets them know that you cared and can bring great peace and comfort.

WHY SHOULD I RECORD MY FAMILY HISTORY?

Don't assume that your family knows your history. For example, does your family know where you were born? The city/town, hospital, home? Do they know how your family came to reside in Canada, your city, or your province? Do your children know their great-grandparents and where they lived?

Below are some reasons people have decided to record their family history; it may have a wider impact than you imagine.

- Discover unknown things about your family.
- It can bring you closer to older relatives and can put you in contact with long-lost relatives.
- Family trees are abstract, and stories add depth.
- Situations, events, and other details can be forgotten over time. It is better to have them recorded.
- Documenting your history creates a first-person narrative about events that have happened in your life.
- Knowing your background can give you a core identity and self-worth.
- Understanding your family history can provide compassion for other family members.
- Writing is reflective, and it can put perspective and bring purpose to your own life.
- Writing is therapeutic.

WHERE DO I GO TO OBTAIN FAMILY INFORMATION?

Death Certificates: Check with your provincial government health department for any deaths registered in the past 70 years. Ensure you have the following information when making inquiries:

- Applicant
- Deceased
- Spouse of deceased
- Mother of deceased
- Father of deceased

Other places to find information:

Extended family members

Church records (births, baptisms, death)

City records/Town Hall

Genetic kits

Provincial health records

Department of Justice

Cemeteries

Heritage websites like Ancestry.com

Local libraries

WHAT SHOULD I INCLUDE, AND HOW FAR BACK SHOULD I GO?

You can include as much or as little as you want! Try to list of all family members as far back as you can remember. Include names, places lived, year born/died, occupation and any other important information. Don't forget to provide information on blended families. Include:

Spouse

Father

Siblings

Children

Aunts

Cousins

Previous spouse

Mother

Grandparents

Children's families (spouses, children)

Uncles

Nieces/Nephews

WHAT OTHER FAMILY DATA SHOULD I INCLUDE?

Again, provide items that may be of interest to other family members. Below are some examples.

- Memorial cards

- Birth announcements

- Graduation ceremony cards

- Diplomas

- Family favorite or traditional recipes

- Family stories/memoirs

- Military information

- Immigration information

- Newspaper clippings

- Other memorabilia

SHOULD I INCLUDE LETTERS FOR MY FAMILY?

Some people like to leave personal letters for their loved ones. These letters are often very personal and are meant to pass on love and thoughts for a time when you can't be there. Sometimes they are meant for special occasions or life milestones, including, but not limited to, graduations, weddings, and births. In place of letters, a digital recording is also an ideal gift.

SUMMARY

Knowing, recording, and preserving your family history, providing other family information, and creating personal letters can directly impact you, your family, and even future generations of people you may never know. It can be the beginning of an exciting and worthwhile journey!

Section 10
PHILANTHROPY AND CHARITY

The old saying goes, "You can't take it with you," and it is true.

WHAT IS PHILANTHROPY?

Philanthropy is defined as a long-term and strategic way of giving back, which often involves making multiple gifts to help people over several years. The focus is on helping people and solving problems and issues over the long-term.

Philanthropy is important because it provides opportunities. It supports projects and endeavors that may be too unpopular or controversial to gain the widespread support of the general public or the government.

WHAT IS CHARITY?

Charity is widespread general support focused on providing immediate relief to people, and it is often driven by emotion.

WHY SHOULD I GIVE?

Donating is a selfless act. One of the major positive effects of donating money to charity is simply feeling good about giving. Being able to give back to those in need helps you achieve a greater sense of personal satisfaction and growth; it feels good to help others. Other reasons are:

- Private giving satisfies deep human needs.
- Every donation makes an impact.
- It strengthens personal values.
- It shows family the importance of generosity.
- It encourages others to do the same.

HOW SHOULD I DECIDE WHAT TO DONATE TO?

Consider the things that drive you or that you are passionate about. What causes do you care about or what has touched your life? There are many charities and organizations available for a wide variety of interests.

HOW CAN I DONATE?

There are many ways to give back.

- **Volunteering your time**: Join an organization, volunteer groups or one of the many non-profit organizations.
- **Donate financially:** You can give financial contributions to a charity or philanthropic cause. You can give on a regular basis, such as monthly or annually.
- **Through your estate**: You can give to a qualified charitable organization in your Will.

WHY SHOULD I DONATE THROUGH MY WILL?

Donations through your Will allow you to give or continue to give to causes that you are passionate about. Gifts that come from your estate are called legacy gifts and are given to charities, philanthropic or non-profit organizations, churches, schools, etc. These gifts may have different names, depending on the organization.

Some of the reasons to consider establishing a legacy gift are as follows:

- If you regularly donate to a charity or have a standing agreement for automatic donations, establishing a legacy gift may be right for you.

- A larger legacy gift can be more impactful than leaving many smaller gifts to multiple charities.

- **Establishing a legacy gift can have major tax benefits for you now or for your estate. It is important to consider when discussing estate and beneficiary tax.** Donations through your Will reduce the taxes owed by your estate. Your estate receives a donation receipt for the gift amount, reducing or even eliminating final taxes. Discuss this and other tax considerations with your tax accountant, financial planner, or a gift planning consultant with the specific charity you have in mind.

- Creating a legacy gift now is less work for your Executor. The gift planning consultant at your charity of choice should handle all the legwork.

- Consider you family's financial situations. Recognize that your adult children are already established, leaving you room to set aside an amount towards something that matters to you.

WHAT SHOULD I DO IF I DECIDE TO LEAVE A LEGACY GIFT?

There are many ways to pre-plan your gift or legacy.

- Research programs to find organizations to match your interests and values.

- Consider establishing legacies during your lifetime to see the benefits. Your legacy will continue through your estate with your donation directed to your existing plan.

- **Talk to the charitable organization.** By pre-planning, the charity will know how to manage your donation once it is received.

- Get your family and friends involved with your legacy.

- **If establishing a legacy gift, be sure that it is mentioned in your Will with the proper legal language.** Include charity organization names, contact information, and terms of the gift.

- Discuss your intentions with your loved ones. Ensure they understand your intentions, and get your family and friends involved with your legacy.

HOW CAN A GIFT PLANNER HELP WITH ESTABLISHING A LEGACY GIFT?

A gift planning consultant from your charity or non-profit has expertise in the area to answer questions you may have. If a gift planning consultant is not available, please consult with an estate lawyer to properly establish the gift.

Some of the areas gift planning consultants can assist are:

- To help you determine if you would like to fund a specific program within the charity.

- If you wish to establish a named legacy.

- To determine if it is better if your gift should be a percentage of your estate or a dollar amount.

- To inform you about tax benefits for you and your estate.

- To provide proper legal wording for your Will.

SUMMARY

The act of helping others, through volunteer work, donating to charities or by leaving a legacy through your estate will improve your sense of well being and create a positive change in the world.

Section 11
OTHER CONSIDERATIONS

In this last section, we look at a few final things for consideration. Please add to this section any details you feel are not covered in *Just in Case*.

11.1 PET CARE

DO YOU OWN PETS?

- Provide names, breeds, and ages.
- List the name of your veterinarian.

- List any pet licence numbers and registered chip information.

WHO WILL TAKE CARE OF YOUR PETS IF YOU ARE ILL?

- Provide name and contact information.

- Have a list of care instructions handy for your caretaker.

- Ensure that this person is aware of their responsibility, and how they will be notified if something happens to you.

WHO WILL TAKE CUSTODY OF YOUR PETS IF YOU PASS?

If this person is different from the pet's caretaker, please provide the following:

- Provide name and contact information.

- Have a list of care instructions handy for your caretaker.

- Ensure that this person is aware of their responsibility, and how they will be notified if something happens to you.

- Pets are legally considered a personal possession and can be indicated within a Will.

11.2 HOUSING

AS YOU AGE, DO YOU PLAN TO STAY IN CURRENT RESIDENCE?

Consider that your home may need renovations or upgrades for accessibility. Decide how easy it will be to make any necessary or required improvements. Discuss with a contractor what may be required and determine the cost to allow for aging in place. Some areas to think about are:

- Wider doorways and hallways to accommodate walkers/wheelchairs.

- Lighting, including access to switches.

- Flooring: Certain carpets may be difficult for walkers/wheelchairs or flooring may be too slippery.

- Cabinets: Heights and accessibility.

- Doorknobs and handles: ease of operation for conditions such as arthritis.

- Stairs/Railings: Are they all in good condition? Do they allow for easy walking and grip?

- Bathroom accessibility: handrail installation, ease of accessibility into tubs and showers, lighting, etc.
- Ramps: Will you require ramps installed in your home or to allow for access into your house?

If you plan to stay in your own home, you should also consider the costs for any at home care that may be required in the event of an illness or injury. A couple of examples of such programs are Home Care and Meals on Wheels.

DO YOU PLAN ON DOWNSIZING?

The following are a few reasons people choose to downsize from their current residence:

Extra cash: Cheaper bills, revenue from sale of home.

Less stress: Less maintenance and upkeep.

Frees up lifestyle: Allows you time to do more of what you love, including travel.

De-clutters: Downsizing means you will have no choice but to sort through your belongings!

Location: Some people move to be closer to family, medical facilities or to a warmer climate.

Rural to urban: Many people move away from the family farm into a town or a city when retiring. Others move to downsize, to be closer to family, or to be closer to services.

New facilities: Some people like the idea and the benefits of a newer home.

DO YOU PLAN ON LIVING IN A SENIOR'S RESIDENCE?

If at any point in your future you are considering moving to a senior's residence, do your research now! Many have long wait lists, have certain requirements, and are all over the map when it comes to pricing. Consider your budget and research your options.

Senior Living Options
These can be referred to as Assisted Living or Independent Living. They are safe living communities in a residential environment for those who may need minimal assistance with daily personalized care. These places can be expensive. Understand what is included in the cost and that most have waiting lists.

Group Homes
These are residential care homes that are privately or corporately run. They might be cheaper and more personalized than assisted living. Some may have nursing staff available. Do your

research to ensure you are going to an accredited home.

Long Term Care Home
Also referred to as a Continuing Care Home, it is for individuals requiring full-time care or a higher level of care requiring nursing or intensive personal assistance. When researching, understand the care home requirements and application processes.

11.3 RETIREMENT PLAN

Many people plan for the financial side of retirement life, but rarely do people consider the non-financial side of retirement. After the first few weeks, some people report feeling a sense of loss. The big question of "Now what?" comes into play.

Consider talking with a counsellor or a retirement coach about retirement life. At the very least, think about how you will manage the following:

MEANING AND PURPOSE

Everyone needs a reason to get up in the morning. Self identity is often wrapped up in careers, and when you no longer have a job to go to, you may feel like you've lost your purpose. Discover or re-discover your passions in life. They can lead you to a whole new chapter!

SOCIALIZE

When we go out of the home to work, we are socializing, whether we realize it or not. Maintaining socialization is vital for a healthy mind and spirit. Think of ways to socialize after you are through with work. Volunteering, becoming a part of a fitness group, helping your family and friends, joining clubs or other organizations are all good examples of ways to maintain social connections.

HEALTH

Keeping up with your health increases the enjoyment of retirement. Don't be afraid of doctors, health appointments, or required surgeries. The longer you put these things off, the worse they can become. Put your health first. Conditions can become more serious and may involve a longer recovery time if ignored.

FITNESS AND ACTIVITY

Make fitness a part of your daily routine. It's important to maintain a healthy lifestyle to support both an aging mind and body, to remain independent for as long as possible. Staying physically active reduces the likeliness of becoming ill; it enhances mobility and flexibility, and assists with memory retention.

NUTRITION

Some people turn to food or baking out of boredom or as a way of distraction, but our bodies do not need the extra calories. Plan your meals accordingly, and think of ways to limit your snacking. Retirement allows you the time to shop and prepare healthy food. If mobility is an issue, there are many local food services available that deliver, which allows you to maintain a nutritious diet. If you don't like cooking for only one or two people, invite over friends and family. Consider starting a dinner party club.

START NOW

If you start these changes prior to retirement, when the time comes, they won't feel so strange.

11.4 DE-CLUTTER

One of the toughest jobs a family confronts after a death or downsizing a loved one is sorting through their belongings. You often hear, "What do we do with this stuff?" Things accumulate over the years and sometimes we are reluctant to de-clutter.

- Look in every room, closet, drawer, and cupboard. If there are items that have not been used in a year or two, get rid of them.

- If you have a special item that someone would treasure, give it to them now and enjoy the satisfaction of giving. Start with giving away a few items and watch the smiles or signs of appreciation. It may encourage you to give more!

- Consider places that help the less fortunate or charities that sell the artifacts, paintings, or special items. Every community has many worthwhile charities.

- Purge records and paper that are outdated (over seven years) and that will be of no use for anyone.

- While you are in the giving mood, if you have extra funds, consider giving some away to a charity or non-profit organization.

11.5 SHARED LEARNING

If you are in a relationship, you may recognize that one person may be better at doing specific tasks than the other. When death or incapacitation occurs suddenly, people can find themselves unprepared, and thrust into new roles and duties.

Responsibilities such as finances, banking, paying bills and looking after annual renewals, cooking, laundry, yard work, and many other chores and obligations involved in making a household run are typically divided. When something happens suddenly, the surviving partner must take on additional new responsibilities on top of their regular tasks, which is incredibly stressful and overwhelming.

Identify those areas that may require some training or exposure to make it easier on the surviving partner when the time comes. Consider writing step-by-step instructions to make beginning a new task easier. You can even take it one step further and identify someone else who can assist in certain areas, bridging the gap.

SUMMARY

As you can see, these are just a few final thoughts on Final Affair planning. They may not seem as important as the earlier identified areas, but they are very important when the time comes. Now is also the time to identify and record anything else that may be necessary to your spouse, partner, or family for when the time comes.

IN CLOSING

Congratulations! You did it. You have made it through planning your affairs! You have accomplished a very large and challenging task and you should be proud.

When you boil it all down, it simply comes to these five points:

1. **Plan your affairs.**

2. **Keep everything up to date.**

3. **Put all documents in one place.**

4. **Let your Executor/Power of Attorney know your plans and where your important documents are.**

5. **Talk to your family about your final affairs.**

Remember

Life brings variety to all.
Every family is different.
Every individual is unique.
Please take the time to consider your personal needs.

Be responsible. Be proactive. And most importantly, be you.

Just in Case.

PART 3

WORKSHEETS

PERSONAL
INFORMATION

1.1 Personal Information

Name: _____

Date Created or Updated:_____

Current Address: _____

Telephone Number: Home:_____   Cell: _____

                                Work: _____

Social Insurance Number (SIN): _____

Driver's License #: _____   Province of Issue: _____

Date of Birth: _____   Place of Birth: _____

Spouse Name: _____

Other: _____

_____

_____

_____

_____

_____

_____

_____

_____

1.2 Medical Information

Name: _____

Date Created or Updated: _____

Provincial Health Card: _____

Family Doctor: _____

Practice Name: _____

Practice Address: _____

City: _____

Organ or Tissue Donor (yes/no): _____

Allergies: _____

_____

_____

_____

Blood Type: _____

Eye glasses/Contacts (yes/no): _____

Eye Doctor Name: _____

Practice Name: _____

Practice Address: _____

City: _____ Province: _____

Pharmacy Name: _____

Pharmacy Location: _____

©2023 *Just in Case* by Elaine Lozinski. This material may not be altered, copied, or translated without permission of the author.

1.2 Medical Information

Current Medication
(Include all medications, vitamins and minerals.)

Medication Name: _____

Dosage: _____

Reason for Medication: _____

Medication Name: _____

Dosage: _____

Reason for Medication: _____

Medication Name: _____

Dosage: _____

Reason for Medication: _____

Medication Name: _____

Dosage: _____

Reason for Medication: _____

Medication Name: _____

Dosage: _____

Reason for Medication: _____

Medication Name: _____

Dosage: _____

Reason for Medication: _____

 ©2023 *Just in Case* by Elaine Lozinski. This material may not be altered, copied, or translated without permission of the author.

1.2 Medical Information

Medical History
(List all surgeries, hospitalizations, procedures, medical conditions, or concerns past and present, etc.)

What: _____

Date: _____

Overseeing
Physician: _____

Physician
Contact Info: _____

_____

Notes: _____

_____

What: _____

Date: _____

Overseeing
Physician: _____

Physician
Contact Info: _____

_____

Notes: _____

_____

What: _____

Date: _____

Overseeing
Physician: _____

Physician
Contact Info: _____

_____

Notes: _____

_____

1.2 Medical Information

Related Family Medical History
List any family medical history such as cancers, diabetes, etc.

_____

_____

_____

_____

_____

_____

_____

_____

_____

_____

_____

_____

_____

_____

_____

_____

_____

_____

_____

©2023 *Just in Case* by Elaine Lozinski. This material may not be altered, copied, or translated without permission of the author.

1.3 Employment Information

Current Employer

Name: _____

Date Created
or Updated: _____

Employer: _____

Title: _____

Employer Address: _____

Employer City: _____ Province: _____

Postal Code: _____

Employer Phone: _____

Employee Number: _____

*For income information see Financial Section

Supervisor or
Contact Email: _____

Company Benefit
Plan: _____

*For futher Benefit Information see Financial Sections

1.3 Employment Information

Past Employment

List all prior employment or provide resume. Include employer name, location, your position and years employed.

Company Name: _____

Address: _____

_____

Title: _____

Years Employed: _____

Company Name: _____

Address: _____

_____

Title: _____

Years Employed: _____

Company Name: _____

Address: _____

_____

Title: _____

Years Employed: _____

Company Name: _____

Address: _____

_____

Title: _____

Years Employed: _____

 ©2023 *Just in Case* by Elaine Lozinski. This material may not be altered, copied, or translated without permission of the author.

1.4 Technology

Name: _____

Date Created
or Updated: _____

Personal Email: _____

Email Provider: _____

Username/Sign on: _____ Password: _____

Home Phone: _____ Voice Mail
Password: _____

Cell Phone: _____ Voice Mail
Password: _____

Usual Location: _____

Desktop Computer: _____ Usual Location: _____

Username/Sign on: _____ Password: _____

Last Back up Date: _____ Notes: _____

Laptop Computer: _____ Usual Location: _____

Username/Sign on: _____ Password: _____

Last Back up Date: _____ Notes: _____

Tablet or Ipad: _____ Usual Location: _____

Username/Sign on: _____ Password: _____

Last Back up Date: _____ Notes: _____

©2023 *Just in Case* by Elaine Lozinski. This material may not be altered, copied, or translated without permission of the author.

1.4-1 Technology: Online Services

Facebook:
Username or Account Number:_____   Password:_____

Linked In:
Username or Account Number:_____   Password:_____

Instagram:
Username or Account Number:_____   Password:_____

Snap Chat:
Username or Account Number:_____   Password:_____

Twitter:
Username or Account Number:_____   Password:_____

Google:
Username or Account Number:_____   Password:_____

Microsoft:
Username or Account Number:_____   Password:_____

Apple Sign-on:
Username or Account Number:_____   Password:_____

Amazon:
Username or Account Number:_____   Password:_____

Go Daddy:
Username or Account Number:_____   Password:_____

Ebay:
Username or Account Number:_____   Password:_____

Hotmail:
Username or Account Number:_____   Password:_____

Pinterest:
Username or Account Number:_____   Password:_____

Other:
Username or Account Number:_____   Password:_____

1.4-1 Technology: Online Services

Other:

Username or Account Number: _____ Password: _____

Other:

Username or Account Number: _____ Password: _____

Other:

Username or Account Number: _____ Password: _____

Other:

Username or Account Number: _____ Password: _____

Other:

Username or Account Number: _____ Password: _____

Other:

Username or Account Number: _____ Password: _____

Other:

Username or Account Number: _____ Password: _____

Other:

Username or Account Number: _____ Password: _____

Other:

Username or Account Number: _____ Password: _____

Other:

Username or Account Number: _____ Password: _____

Other:

Username or Account Number: _____ Password: _____

Other:

Username or Account Number: _____ Password: _____

Other:

Username or Account Number: _____ Password: _____

 ©2023 *Just in Case* by Elaine Lozinski. This material may not be altered, copied, or translated without permission of the author.

1.5 Military Service Information

Name: _____

Date Created
or Updated: _____

Branch: _____

Unit or Regiment: _____

Current Rank: _____

Date Entered Service: _____

Place: _____

Date of Discharge: _____

Place: _____

Contact Name: _____

Contact Phone
Number: _____

Contact Email: _____

Other Information: _____

_____

_____

_____

_____

_____

_____

_____

1.6 Legal Information

Name: _____

Date Created
or Updated: _____

Lawyer: _____

Firm Name: _____

Firm Address: _____

City: _____ Province: _____

Phone: _____

Type: (Family Law,
Estate, etc.): _____

Notes: _____

_____

_____

Lawyer: _____

Firm Name: _____

Firm Address: _____

City: _____ Province: _____

Phone: _____

Type: (Family Law,
Estate, etc.): _____

Notes: _____

_____

©2023 *Just in Case* by Elaine Lozinski. This material may not be altered, copied, or translated without permission of the author.

1.7 Personal Information: Other

Name: _____

Date Created or Updated: _____

Education

High School: _____

Post-Secondary: _____

Certificate, Diploma, etc.: _____

Designation, Accreditation, Other Credentials

Type: _____

Professional Association: _____

Governing Regulatory Body: _____

Contact: _____

Combinations and Codes

Safe Location: _____

Safe Combination: _____

House/Garage Door
Combinations/Alarm Codes: _____

Other Combination Locks: _____

Memberships, Registrations, Etc.

Magazine Subscriptions: _____

Social Organizations: _____

Memberships:
(Costco, Co-ops, etc.) _____

Registrations:
(Firearm, Jewelry, etc.) _____

©2023 *Just in Case* by Elaine Lozinski. This material may not be altered, copied, or translated without permission of the author.

1.7 Personal Information: Other

Post Office Box

PO Box Number: _____

Location of Box: _____

Location of Key: _____

Reward Programs

Name: _____

Type (retail, travel, etc.): _____

Other Information
List any other information you feel may be helpful to someone looking after your affairs.

_____

_____

_____

_____

_____

_____

_____

_____

_____

_____

_____

_____

 ©2023 *Just in Case* by Elaine Lozinski. This material may not be altered, copied, or translated without permission of the author.

CONTACT LISTS

2.1 Personal Contacts
In case of Emergency, Death, or First to Know

Name: _____

Date Created
or Updated: _____

Contact Name: _____

Telephone: _____ Cell: _____

Email: _____

Address: _____

_____

Relationship: _____

Chain (This person is to notify): _____

Notes: _____

_____

Contact Name: _____

Telephone: _____ Cell: _____

Email: _____

Address: _____

_____

Relationship: _____

Chain (This person is to notify): _____

Notes: _____

_____

2.1 Personal Contacts
In case of Emergency, Death, or First to Know

Contact Name: _____

Telephone: _____ Cell: _____

Email: _____

Address: _____

_____

Relationship: _____

Chain (This person is to notify): _____

Notes: _____

_____

Contact Name: _____

Telephone: _____ Cell: _____

Email: _____

Address: _____

_____

Relationship: _____

Chain (This person is to notify): _____

Notes: _____

_____

 ©2023 *Just in Case* by Elaine Lozinski. This material may not be altered, copied, or translated without permission of the author.

2.2 Contacts: Other

Name: _____

Date Created or Updated: _____

Checklist	Check	Phone Number or Email Address
Banks		
Credit Card Companies		
Investment Firms		
Insurance Companies		
Provincial Health Insurance		
Vehicle Insurance		
Land Titles		
Benefit Companies		
City/Municipal Property Tax		

Government of Canada:

CRA		
Old Age Security (OAS)		
Canada Pension Plan (CPP)		
Personal Pension Plan		
Passport		

Utility Companies:

Power		
Energy		
Phone		
Internet		
Water		
Other		

Social Organizations:

Clubs		
Charity Work		
Fraternity/Sorority		
Church		
Community Organization		

2.2 Contacts: Other

Name: _____

Date Created or Updated: _____

Checklist	Check	Phone Number or Email Address
Professional and Personal Memberships:		
Accreditations		
Board Membership		
Team Sports Member		
Gym Membership		
Co-ops		
Credit Unions		
Others		

Registrations:

Firearm		
Artwork		
Jewelry		
Other		

Reward Programs:

Hotel		
Travel		
Retail		
Other		

Personal Services:

Hair Stylist		
Esthetician		
Yard Service		
House Cleaning Service		
Other		

Online Services:
See listing under Personal Information - Technology

Magazine Subscriptions		
Charitable Donations		
Other		

©2023 *Just in Case* by Elaine Lozinski. This material may not be altered, copied, or translated without permission of the author.

FINANCIAL INFORMATION

3.1-1 Financial Institutions

Name: _____

Date Created
or Updated: _____

Bank Name: _____

Branch Address: _____

Telephone Number: _____

Online Username: _____

Account Information

Account Number: _____

Account Type
(Savings, Chequing): _____ Approximate Value: _____

Ownership (Sole or Joint): _____ Name of Co-owner: _____

Account General Purpose: _____

Notes: _____

_____

_____

Account Number: _____

Account Type
(Savings, Chequing): _____ Approximate Value: _____

Ownership (Sole or Joint): _____ Name of Co-owner: _____

Account General Purpose: _____

Notes: _____

_____

_____

3.1-1 Financial Institutions

Account Number: _____

Account Type
(Savings, Chequing): _____ Approximate Value: _____

Ownership (Sole or Joint): _____ Name of Co-owner: _____

Account General Purpose: _____

Notes: _____

_____

_____

Account Number: _____

Account Type
(Savings, Chequing): _____ Approximate Value: _____

Ownership (Sole or Joint): _____ Name of Co-owner: _____

Account General Purpose: _____

Notes: _____

_____

_____

Account Number: _____

Account Type
(Savings, Chequing): _____ Approximate Value: _____

Ownership (Sole or Joint): _____ Name of Co-owner: _____

Account General Purpose: _____

Notes: _____

_____

©2023 *Just in Case* by Elaine Lozinski. This material may not be altered, copied, or translated without permission of the author.

3.1-2 Auto Charges or Deposits

Name: _____

Date Created or Updated: _____

Bank or Credit Card Name: _____

Account or Card Number: _____

Amount: _____

Withdrawal or Charge Date: _____

Date of Completion: _____

Notes: _____

_____

Bank or Credit Card Name: _____

Account or Card Number: _____

Amount: _____

Withdrawal or Charge Date: _____

Date of Completion: _____

Notes: _____

_____

Bank or Credit Card Name: _____

Account or Card Number: _____

Amount: _____

Withdrawal or Charge Date: _____

Date of Completion: _____

Notes: _____

_____

©2023 *Just in Case* by Elaine Lozinski. This material may not be altered, copied, or translated without permission of the author.

3.1-2 Auto Charges or Deposits

Bank or Credit Card Name: _____

Account or Card Number: _____

Amount: _____

Withdrawal or Charge Date: _____

Date of Completion: _____

Notes: _____

_____

Bank or Credit Card Name: _____

Account or Card Number: _____

Amount: _____

Withdrawal or Charge Date: _____

Date of Completion: _____

Notes: _____

_____

Bank or Credit Card Name: _____

Account or Card Number: _____

Amount: _____

Withdrawal or Charge Date: _____

Date of Completion: _____

Notes: _____

_____

 ©2023 *Just in Case* by Elaine Lozinski. This material may not be altered, copied, or translated without permission of the author.

3.1-3 Debit and Credit Cards

Name: _____

Date Created or Updated: _____

Bank or Credit Card Name: _____

Card Number: _____

PIN: _____

Password: _____

Card Limit: _____

Promotion or Reward Type: _____

Notes: _____

Bank or Credit Card Name: _____

Card Number: _____

PIN: _____

Password: _____

Card Limit: _____

Promotion or Reward Type: _____

Notes: _____

Bank or Credit Card Name: _____

Card Number: _____

PIN: _____

Password: _____

Card Limit: _____

Promotion or Reward Type: _____

Notes: _____

©2023 *Just in Case* by Elaine Lozinski. This material may not be altered, copied, or translated without permission of the author.

3.1-3 Debit and Credit Cards

Bank or Credit Card Name: _____

Card Number: _____

PIN: _____

Password: _____

Card Limit: _____

Promotion or Reward Type: _____

Notes: _____

Bank or Credit Card Name: _____

Card Number: _____

PIN: _____

Password: _____

Card Limit: _____

Promotion or Reward Type: _____

Notes: _____

Bank or Credit Card Name: _____

Card Number: _____

PIN: _____

Password: _____

Card Limit: _____

Promotion or Reward Type: _____

Notes: _____

_____

 ©2023 *Just in Case* by Elaine Lozinski. This material may not be altered, copied, or translated without permission of the author.

3.1-4 Safety Deposit Box

Name: _____

Date Created
or Updated: _____

Financial Institution: _____

Branch Address: _____

Telephone Number: _____

Box Number: _____

Key Location: _____

Ownership (Sole or Joint): _____   Co-owner: _____

Contents: _____

Notes: _____

_____

_____

_____

_____

_____

_____

_____

_____

_____

_____

_____

3.2-1 Income

Name: _____

Date Created
or Updated: _____

Source

Item (Pay cheque, pension,
government program, etc.): _____

Amount: _____ Deposit Date: _____

Deposit Account Number: _____

Financial Institution: _____

Financial Branch Address: _____

Notes: _____

_____

_____

_____

_____

Source

Item (Pay cheque, pension,
government program, etc): _____

Amount: _____ Deposit Date: _____

Deposit Account Number: _____

Financial Institution: _____

Financial Branch Address: _____

Notes: _____

_____

_____

©2023 *Just in Case* by Elaine Lozinski. This material may not be altered, copied, or translated without permission of the author.

3.2-2 Investments/Trusts

Name: _____

Date Created
or Updated: _____

Investment Firm

Firm Name: _____

Firm Address: _____

Broker Name: _____

Telephone Number: _____

Access ID,
Online Username, etc.: _____ Password/PIN: _____

Account Information

Account Number: _____

Investment Type
(RRSP, TFSA, Mutual, etc.): _____

Approximate Value: _____

Ownership (Sole or Joint): _____ Name of Co-owner: _____

Beneficiary (if applicable): _____

Notes: _____

_____

_____

_____

_____

_____

3.2-2 Investments/Trusts

Account Information

Account Number: _____

Investment Type
(RRSP, TFSA, Mutual, etc.): _____

Approximate Value: _____

Ownership (Sole or Joint): _____ Name of Co-owner: _____

Beneficiary (if applicable): _____

Notes: _____

_____

_____

_____

_____

Account Information

Account Number: _____

Investment Type
(RRSP, TFSA, Mutual, etc.): _____

Approximate Value: _____

Ownership (Sole or Joint): _____ Name of Co-owner: _____

Beneficiary (if applicable): _____

Notes: _____

_____

_____

_____

_____

    ©2023 *Just in Case* by Elaine Lozinski. This material may not be altered, copied, or translated without permission of the author.

3.3-3 Tax Returns

Name: _____

Date Created
or Updated: _____

Prepared by:
Name/Accountant: _____

Firm Name
(if applicable): _____

Address: _____

_____

Phone Number: _____

Date Filed: _____

Location of Return: _____

Notes: _____

_____

_____

_____

_____

_____

_____

_____

©2023 *Just in Case* by Elaine Lozinski. This material may not be altered, copied, or translated without permission of the author.

3.3-1 Mortgage

Name: _____

Date Created
or Updated: _____

Mortgage

Financial Institution: _____

Branch Address: _____

Telephone Number: _____

Owner Name(s): _____

Property Address: _____

Mortgage Balance: _____

Payment Amount: _____ Payment Date: _____

Account Number: _____

Mortgage Type: _____

Interest Rate: _____

Term: _____

Life Insured (yes/no): _____

Notes: _____

_____

_____

_____

_____

_____

_____

3.3-2 Loans

Loans

Financial Institution: _____

Branch Address: _____

Telephone Number: _____

Owner Name(s): _____

Loan Purpose: _____

Approximate Loan
Balance: _____

Payment Amount: _____ Payment Date: _____

Account Number: _____

Interest Rate: _____

Term: _____

Life Insured (yes/no): _____

Notes: _____

_____

_____

_____

_____

_____

_____

_____

_____

©2023 *Just in Case* by Elaine Lozinski. This material may not be altered, copied, or translated without permission of the author.

3.3-3 Support

Child Support/Alimony

Financial Institution: _____

Branch Address: _____

Telephone Number: _____

Support Type: _____

Support Amount: _____

Payment Amount: _____ Payment Date: _____

Recipient Name: _____

Expiration Terms: _____

Notes: _____

_____

_____

_____

_____

_____

_____

_____

_____

_____

_____

_____

3.3-4 Lease Agreements

Name: _____

Date Created
or Updated: _____

Lessor Name: _____

Lessor Address: _____

Telephone Number: _____

Lease for: _____

Lease Number: _____

Lessee Names: _____

_____

Lessee Phone: _____

Property Location: _____

_____

Payment Date: _____

Payment Amount: _____

Term: _____

Deposit Amount: _____

How payment is made: _____

Location of Agreement: _____

Notes: _____

_____

_____

©2023 *Just in Case* by Elaine Lozinski. This material may not be altered, copied, or translated without permission of the author.

3.3-5 Liabilities: Other

Other Liabilities/Financial Responsibilities

Type: _____

Financial Institution: _____

Branch Address: _____

Telephone Number: _____

Owner Name(s): _____

_____

Approximate Balance: _____

Payment Amount: _____ Payment Date: _____

Account Number: _____

Notes: _____

_____

Type: _____

Financial Institution: _____

Branch Address: _____

Telephone Number: _____

Owner Name(s): _____

_____

Approximate Balance: _____

Payment Amount: _____ Payment Date: _____

Account Number: _____

Notes: _____

_____

_____

3.4-1 Power and Energy

Name: _____

Date Created
or Updated: _____

Power Provider: _____

Username: _____ Password: _____

Other Account Holder: _____

Account Number: _____

Amount (approximate): _____

How payment is made: _____

Notes: _____

_____

Energy Provider: _____

Username: _____ Password: _____

Other Account Holder: _____

Account Number: _____

Amount (approximate): _____

How payment is made: _____

Notes: _____

_____

©2023 *Just in Case* by Elaine Lozinski. This material may not be altered, copied, or translated without permission of the author.

3.4-2 Phone Services

Telephone Provider: _____

Username: _____ Password: _____

Other Account Holder: _____

Account Number: _____

Amount (approximate): _____

How payment is made: _____

Notes: _____

_____

Cellular Provider: _____

Username: _____ Password: _____

Other Account Holder: _____

Account Number: _____

Amount (approximate): _____

How payment is made: _____

Notes: _____

_____

3.4-3 Water and Municipal/City Tax

Water Provider: _____

Username: _____ Password: _____

Other Account Holder: _____

Account Number: _____

Amount (approximate): _____

How payment is made: _____

Notes: _____

_____

Municipal or City Tax: _____

Username: _____ Password: _____

Other Account Holder: _____

Account Number: _____

Amount (approximate): _____

How payment is made: _____

Notes: _____

_____

3.4-4 Internet and TV Streaming Services

Internet Service Provider: _____

Username: _____ Password: _____

Other Account Holder: _____

Account Number: _____

Amount (approximate): _____

How payment is made: _____

Notes: _____

_____

Cable Service Provider: _____

Username: _____ Password: _____

Other Account Holder: _____

Account Number: _____

Amount (approximate): _____

How payment is made: _____

Notes: _____

_____

3.4-4 Internet and TV Streaming Services

Satellite Service Provider: _____

Username: _____ Password: _____

Other Account Holder: _____

Account Number: _____

Amount (approximate): _____

How payment is made: _____

Notes: _____

Streaming Service Provider: _____

Username: _____ Password: _____

Other Account Holder: _____

Account Number: _____

Amount (approximate): _____

How payment is made: _____

Notes: _____

Streaming Service Provider: _____

Username: _____ Password: _____

Other Account Holder: _____

Account Number: _____

Amount (approximate): _____

How payment is made: _____

Notes: _____

 ©2023 *Just in Case* by Elaine Lozinski. This material may not be altered, copied, or translated without permission of the author.

3.4-5 Utilities: Other

Utilities Other: _____

Username: _____ Password: _____

Other Account Holder: _____

Account Number: _____

Amount (approximate): _____

How payment is made: _____

Notes: _____

_____

Utilities Other: _____

Username: _____ Password: _____

Other Account Holder: _____

Account Number: _____

Amount (approximate): _____

How payment is made: _____

Notes: _____

_____

3.4-5 Utilities: Other

Utilities Other: _____

Username: _____ Password: _____

Other Account Holder: _____

Account Number: _____

Amount (approximate): _____

How payment is made: _____

Notes: _____

_____

Utilities Other: _____

Username: _____ Password: _____

Other Account Holder: _____

Account Number: _____

Amount (approximate): _____

How payment is made: _____

Notes: _____

_____

 ©2023 *Just in Case* by Elaine Lozinski. This material may not be altered, copied, or translated without permission of the author.

3.5-1 Home

Name: _____

Date Created
or Updated: _____

Civic Location: _____

City, Province: _____

Legal Property Address
(Lot #): _____

Land Location: _____

_____

Date Purchased: _____

Names on Registration
(Ownership): _____

Registration Number: _____

Estimated/Appraised
Current Market Value: _____

Mortgaged (yes/no): _____
*For further information see section 3.3-1 Mortgage

Listed in Last Will and Testament (yes/no): _____

Notes: _____

_____

_____

_____

_____

_____

3.5-2 Farm Land

Name: _____

Date Created
or Updated: _____

*Please consult a professional about Farm Succession Planning

RM, Province: _____

Land Location(s): _____

_____

Home Quarter Location: _____

Date Purchased: _____

Names on Registration
(Ownership): _____

Registration Number: _____

Estimated/Appraised
Current Market Value: _____

Mortgaged (yes/no): _____
*For further information see section 3.3-1 Mortgage

Listed in Last Will and Testament (yes/no): _____

Succession Plan Established (yes/no): _____

Notes: _____

_____

_____

_____

_____

3.5-3 Business

Name: _____

Date Created or Updated: _____
*Please consult a professional about Business Succession Planning

Business Name (Operating Name): _____

Registered Name
(if different from operating name): _____

Owner(s): _____

_____

Partner(s): _____

_____

_____

RM, Province: _____

Land Location(s): _____

_____

Date Purchased: _____

Names on Registration
(Ownership): _____

Registration Number: _____

Estimated/Appraised
Current Market Value: _____

Mortgaged (yes/no): _____
*For further information see section 3.3-1 Mortgage

Listed in Last Will and Testament (yes/no): _____

Succession Plan Established (yes/no): _____

©2023 *Just in Case* by Elaine Lozinski. This material may not be altered, copied, or translated without permission of the author.

3.5-4 Vacation Property

Name: _____

Date Created
or Updated: _____

Civic Location: _____

City, Province: _____

Legal Property Address
(Lot #): _____

Land Location: _____

_____

Date Purchased: _____

Names on Registration
(Ownership): _____

Registration Number: _____

Estimated/Appraised
Current Market Value: _____

Mortgaged (yes/no): _____
*For further information see section 3.3-1 Mortgage

Listed in Last Will and Testament (yes/no): _____

Notes: _____

_____

_____

_____

_____

3.5-5 Real Estate

Name: _____

Date Created
or Updated: _____

Civic Location: _____

City, Province: _____

Legal Property Address
(Lot #): _____

Land Location: _____

_____

Date Purchased: _____

Names on Registration
(Ownership): _____

Registration Number: _____

Estimated/Appraised
Current Market Value: _____

Mortgaged (yes/no): _____
*For further information see section 3.3-1 Mortgage

Listed in Last Will and Testament (yes/no): _____

Notes: _____

_____

_____

_____

_____

_____

3.5-6 Vehicle(s)

Name: _____

Date Created
or Updated: _____

Vehicle Make: _____ Vehicle Year: _____

Vehicle Model: _____

VIN Number: _____

Date of Purchase: _____

Approximate Current
Value: _____

Location of Vehicle: _____

Registered Owner: _____

Registration Number: _____

License Plate Number: _____

Outstanding Loan (yes/no): _____
*For further information see section 3.3-2 Loans

Listed in Last Will and Testament (yes/no): _____

Notes: _____

_____

_____

_____

_____

_____

3.5-7 Recreational Vehicle(s)

Name: _____

Date Created
or Updated: _____

Type (Boat, Snowmobile,
Motorcycle, ATV, etc.): _____

Vehicle Make: _____ Vehicle Year: _____

Vehicle Model: _____

VIN Number: _____

Date of Purchase: _____

Approximate Current
Value: _____

Location of Vehicle: _____

Registered Owner: _____

Registration Number: _____

License Plate Number: _____

Outstanding Loan (yes/no): _____
*For further information see section 3.3-2 Loans

Listed in Last Will and Testament (yes/no): _____

Notes: _____

_____

_____

_____

_____

_____

3.5-8 Major Assets: Other

Name: _____

Date Created
or Updated: _____

Type: _____

Description: _____

_____

_____

_____

Approximate Current
Value: _____

Location: _____

Registered Owner: _____

Registration Number: _____

_____

Outstanding Loan (yes/no): _____
*For further information see section 3.3-2 Loans

Listed in Last Will and Testament (yes/no): _____

Notes: _____

_____

_____

_____

_____

_____

3.5-9 Major Assets: Notes

Name: _____

Date Created
or Updated: _____

Asset Type: _____

Notes: _____

_____

_____

_____

_____

_____

_____

_____

_____

_____

_____

_____

_____

_____

_____

3.6-1 Life Insurance

Name: _____

Date Created or Updated: _____

Insurance Type: _____

Policy Holder Name: _____

Broker Name: _____

Broker Address: _____

Phone Number: _____

Firm or Company Name: _____

Firm Address: _____

Phone Number: _____

Representative Name: _____

Access ID, Online
Username, etc.: _____ Password/PIN: _____

Ownership
(Sole or Joint): _____ Name of Co-owner: _____

Beneficiaries: _____

Expiry Date: _____

Account Number: _____

Coverage Amount: _____

Premium Amount: _____

Premium Payment Date: _____

How payment is made: _____

Policy Location: _____

Notes: _____

3.6-2 Accidental Insurance

Name: _____

Date Created or Updated: _____

Insurance Type: _____

Policy Holder Name: _____

Broker Name: _____

Broker Address: _____

Phone Number: _____

Firm or Company Name: _____

Firm Address: _____

Phone Number: _____

Representative Name: _____

Access ID, Online
Username, etc.: _____   Password/PIN: _____

Ownership
(Sole or Joint): _____   Name of Co-owner: _____

Beneficiaries: _____

Expiry Date: _____

Account Number: _____

Coverage Amount: _____

Premium Amount: _____

Premium Payment Date: _____

How payment is made: _____

Policy Location: _____

Notes: _____

©2023 *Just in Case* by Elaine Lozinski. This Material may not be altered, copied, or translated without permission of the author.

3.6-3 Disability Insurance

Name: _____

Date Created or Updated: _____

Insurance Type: _____

Policy Holder Name: _____

Broker Name: _____

Broker Address: _____

Phone Number: _____

Firm or Company Name: _____

Firm Address: _____

Phone Number: _____

Representative Name: _____

Access ID, Online
Username, etc.: _____ Password/PIN: _____

Ownership
(Sole or Joint): _____ Name of Co-owner: _____

Beneficiaries: _____

Expiry Date: _____

Account Number: _____

Coverage Amount: _____

Premium Amount: _____

Premium Payment Date: _____

How payment is made: _____

Policy Location: _____

Notes: _____

©2023 *Just in Case* by Elaine Lozinski. This material may not be altered, copied, or translated without permission of the author.

3.6-4 Medical Insurance

Name: _____

Date Created or Updated: _____

Insurance Type: _____

Policy Holder Name: _____

Broker Name: _____

Broker Address: _____

Phone Number: _____

Firm or Company Name: _____

Firm Address: _____

Phone Number: _____

Representative Name: _____

Access ID, Online
Username, etc.: _____ Password/PIN: _____

Ownership
(Sole or Joint): _____ Name of Co-owner: _____

Beneficiaries: _____

Expiry Date: _____

Account Number: _____

Coverage Amount: _____

Premium Amount: _____

Premium Payment Date: _____

How payment is made: _____

Policy Location: _____

Notes: _____

3.6-5 Home Insurance

Name: _____

Date Created or Updated: _____

Insurance Type: _____

Policy Holder Name: _____

Broker Name: _____

Broker Address: _____

Phone Number: _____

Firm or Company Name: _____

Firm Address: _____

Phone Number: _____

Representative Name: _____

Access ID, Online
Username, etc.: _____   Password/PIN: _____

Ownership
(Sole or Joint): _____   Name of Co-owner: _____

Beneficiaries: _____

Expiry Date: _____

Account Number: _____

Coverage Amount: _____

Premium Amount: _____

Premium Payment Date: _____

How payment is made: _____

Policy Location: _____

Notes: _____

3.6-6 Vacation Home Insurance

Name: _____

Date Created or Updated: _____

Insurance Type: _____

Policy Holder Name: _____

Broker Name: _____

Broker Address: _____

Phone Number: _____

Firm or Company Name: _____

Firm Address: _____

Phone Number: _____

Representative Name: _____

Access ID, Online
Username, etc.: _____ Password/PIN: _____

Ownership
(Sole or Joint): _____ Name of Co-owner: _____

Beneficiaries: _____

Expiry Date: _____

Account Number: _____

Coverage Amount: _____

Premium Amount: _____

Premium Payment Date: _____

How payment is made: _____

Policy Location: _____

Notes: _____

3.6-7 Farm/Crop Insurance

Name: _____

Date Created or Updated: _____

Insurance Type: _____

Policy Holder Name: _____

Broker Name: _____

Broker Address: _____

Phone Number: _____

Firm or Company Name: _____

Firm Address: _____

Phone Number: _____

Representative Name: _____

Access ID, Online
Username, etc.: _____   Password/PIN: _____

Ownership
(Sole or Joint): _____   Name of Co-owner: _____

Beneficiaries: _____

Expiry Date: _____

Account Number: _____

Coverage Amount: _____

Premium Amount: _____

Premium Payment Date: _____

How payment is made: _____

Land Description or Location: _____

Policy Location: _____

©2023 *Just in Case* by Elaine Lozinski. This material may not be altered, copied, or translated without permission of the author.

3.6-8 Vehicle Insurance

Name: _____

Date Created or Updated: _____

Insurance Type: _____

Policy Holder Name: _____

Broker Name: _____

Broker Address: _____

Phone Number: _____

Firm or Company Name: _____

Firm Address: _____

Phone Number: _____

Representative Name: _____

Access ID, Online
Username, etc.: _____ Password/PIN: _____

Ownership
(Sole or Joint): _____ Name of Co-owner: _____

Beneficiaries: _____

Expiry Date: _____

Account Number: _____

Coverage Amount: _____

Premium Amount: _____

Premium Payment Date: _____

How payment is made: _____

Policy Location: _____

Notes: _____

©2023 *Just in Case* by Elaine Lozinski. This material may not be altered, copied, or translated without permission of the author.

3.6-9 Recreational Vehicle(s) Insurance

Name: _____

Date Created or Updated: _____

Insurance Type: _____

Policy Holder Name: _____

Broker Name: _____

Broker Address: _____

Phone Number: _____

Firm or Company Name: _____

Firm Address: _____

Phone Number: _____

Representative Name: _____

Access ID, Online
Username, etc.: _____ Password/PIN: _____

Ownership
(Sole or Joint): _____ Name of Co-owner: _____

Beneficiaries: _____

Expiry Date: _____

Account Number: _____

Coverage Amount: _____

Premium Amount: _____

Premium Payment Date: _____

How payment is made: _____

Policy Location: _____

Notes: _____

©2023 *Just in Case* by Elaine Lozinski. This material may not be altered, copied, or translated without permission of the author.

3.6-10 Insurance: Other

Name: _____

Date Created or Updated: _____

Insurance Type: _____

Policy Holder Name: _____

Broker Name: _____

Broker Address: _____

Phone Number: _____

Firm or Company Name: _____

Firm Address: _____

Phone Number: _____

Representative Name: _____

Access ID, Online
Username, etc.: _____ Password/PIN: _____

Ownership
(Sole or Joint): _____ Name of Co-owner: _____

Beneficiaries: _____

Expiry Date: _____

Account Number: _____

Coverage Amount: _____

Premium Amount: _____

Premium Payment Date: _____

How payment is made: _____

Policy Location: _____

Notes: _____

3.6-11 Notes

Name: _____

Date Created or Updated: _____

Insurance Type: _____

Notes: _____

_____

_____

_____

_____

_____

_____

_____

_____

_____

_____

_____

_____

_____

_____

_____

_____

_____

POWER OF ATTORNEY

4.1 Power of Attorney

Name: _____

Date Created
or Updated: _____

Location of Power of
Attorney Papers: _____

Power of Attorney Type: (Personal, Property, Sole, Joint or Successive) _____

Power of Attorney Granted to: _____

Phone Number: _____ Email: _____

Address: _____

_____

Power of Attorney Type: (Personal, Property, Sole, Joint or Successive) _____

Power of Attorney Granted to: _____

Phone Number: _____ Email: _____

Address: _____

_____

Power of Attorney Type: (Personal, Property, Sole, Joint or Successive) _____

Power of Attorney Granted to: _____

Phone Number: _____ Email: _____

Address: _____

Notes: _____

_____

_____

HEALTH CARE
DIRECTIVE

5.1 Health Care Directive

Name: _____

Date Created
or Updated: _____

Location of Power of
Attorney Papers: _____

Health Care Directive Type: (Sole, Alternate, or Joint) _____

Proxy Granted to: _____

Phone Number: _____ Email: _____

Address: _____

_____

Health Care Directive Type: (Sole, Alternate, or Joint) _____

Proxy Granted to: _____

Phone Number: _____ Email: _____

Address: _____

_____

Health Care Directive Type: (Sole, Alternate, or Joint) _____

Proxy Granted to: _____

Phone Number: _____ Email: _____

Address: _____

Notes: _____

_____

_____

©2023 *Just in Case* by Elaine Lozinski. This material may not be altered, copied, or translated without permission of the author.

5.1-1 Health Care Directive: Notes

Notes

_____

_____

_____

_____

_____

_____

_____

_____

_____

_____

_____

_____

_____

_____

_____

_____

_____

_____

_____

_____

©2023 _Just in Case_ by Elaine Lozinski. This material may not be altered, copied, or translated without permission of the author.

WILL AND ESTATE
INFORMATION

6.1 Will and Estate Information

Name: _____

Date Created
or Updated: _____

**Location of Last
Will and Testament:** _____

Lawyer Name: _____

Law Firm: _____

Firm Address: _____

_____

Firm Telephone: _____

Executor Name: _____

Type: (Sole, Alternate, or Joint) _____

Phone: _____ Email: _____

Address: _____

_____

Executor Name: _____

Type: (Sole, Alternate, or Joint) _____

Phone: _____ Email: _____

Address: _____

_____

Executor Name: _____

Type: (Sole, Alternate, or Joint) _____

Phone: _____ Email: _____

Address: _____

_____

©2023 *Just in Case* by Elaine Lozinski. This material may not be altered, copied, or translated without permission of the author.

6.2 Will and Estate: Notes

Notes

_____

_____

_____

_____

_____

_____

_____

_____

_____

_____

_____

_____

_____

_____

_____

_____

_____

_____

_____

_____

©2023 *Just in Case* by Elaine Lozinski. This material may not be altered, copied, or translated without permission of the author.

6.3 Letter of Intent

For the guidance of my Executors, trustees and my family members, my personal belongings are to be distributed in the following manner:

	Item Description	Item Location	Recipient Name	Recipient Address	Witness Initial
1.					
2.					
3.					
4.					
5.					
6.					
7.					
8.					
9.					
10.					
11.					
12.					
13.					
14.					
15.					
16.					
17.					
18.					
19.					
20.					

_____
Signature(s) of Grantor

_____
Date

_____
Signature of Witness

_____
Date

©2023 *Just in Case* by Elaine Lozinski. This material may not be altered, copied, or translated without permission of the author.

FUNERAL/MEMORIAL ARRANGEMENTS

7.1 Funeral Home Information

Name: _____

Date Created
or Updated: _____

Funeral or Memorial Arrangements Made (yes/no): _____

Funeral Home: _____

Funeral Home
Address: _____

_____

Telephone: _____

Payment Plan or Funeral
Insurance Provider: _____

_____

Required Information for Funeral Home

Funeral home pre-arrangements should cover all information. Please review to confirm.

Full name
(including any middle names): _____

Social Insurance Number (SIN): _____

Date of Birth: _____ Place of Birth: _____

Birth Certificate Location: _____

Spouse Name: _____

Executor Name(s): _____

Executor(s) Contact Information: _____

Main Contact for Family: _____

Family Contact Information: _____

©2023 *Just in Case* by Elaine Lozinski. This material may not be altered, copied, or translated without permission of the author.

7.1 Funeral Home Information

Father's Full Name: _____

Mother's Full Name
including maiden name: _____

Highest Level of Education: _____

Occupation: _____

Recent Photograph Location: _____

Other: _____

_____

_____

_____

_____

_____

_____

_____

_____

_____

_____

_____

_____

_____

 ©2023 *Just in Case* by Elaine Lozinski. This material may not be altered, copied, or translated without permission of the author.

7.2 Funeral/Memorial Service

Name: _____

Date Created
or Updated: _____

Funeral Home: _____

Funeral Home
Address: _____

_____

Telephone: _____

Funeral home pre-arrangements should include the following information. Please review to confirm.

Service Type: _____
(Traditional funeral, memorial service, casual gathering, etc.)

Service Location: _____

Officiate: _____

Viewing (yes/no): _____

Music Selections: _____

_____

Reading Selections
(Readings, Prayers, Bible Verses, etc): _____

_____

Location of Photos (for memorial card,
feature photo, slide presentations): _____

Eulogy written by: _____

Eulogy delivered by: _____

Pallbearers: _____

_____

_____

©2023 *Just in Case* by Elaine Lozinski. This material may not be altered, copied, or translated without permission of the author.

7.2 Funeral/Memorial Service

Flower Preference: _____

Charitable Donation
Preference: _____

After Service
Gathering (yes/no): _____

Location: _____

Person Responsible: _____

Notes: _____

_____

_____

_____

_____

_____

_____

_____

_____

_____

_____

_____

_____

_____

_____

_____

   ©2023 *Just in Case* by Elaine Lozinski. This material may not be altered, copied, or translated without permission of the author.

7.3 Interment

Name: _____

Date Created
or Updated: _____

Funeral Home: _____

Funeral Home
Address: _____

_____

Telephone: _____

Funeral home pre-arrangements should include the following information. Please review to confirm.

Transportation required: _____

Embalming or other preparation: _____

Burial or Cremation: _____

Cremation

Urn Preference: _____

Ashes Buried
or Scattered: _____

Location (Plot,
Columbarium, or other): _____

Notes: _____

_____

_____

_____

_____

_____

_____

7.3 Interment

Burial

Casket Preference: _____

Clothes and Jewelry
Preference: _____

Interment Location: _____

Funeral Marker Preference:
(Headstone, marker or monument, etc.): _____

Marker Style: _____

Marker Material: _____

Epitaph: _____

_____

Notes: _____

_____

_____

_____

_____

_____

_____

_____

_____

_____

_____

_____

_____

_____

 ©2023 *Just in Case* by Elaine Lozinski. This material may not be altered, copied, or translated without permission of the author.

7.4 Obituary/Eulogy

Name: _____

Date Created
or Updated: _____

*Please consider publication costs when creating the obituary. Save more information for the eulogy.
*Please indicate where required information is located for the obituary.

Obituary Writer: _____

Person to Deliver Eulogy: _____

Information Required for Obituary

Full Name: _____

Date of Birth: _____

Place of Birth: _____

Name of Parents: _____

Predeceased by: _____

_____

_____

_____

Survived by:
Please list family members as you would like them to appear in the obituary. **Ensure spelling is correct.**
Include spouse, children, children's spouses, grandchildren (including step-children), parents, etc.
Please ensure to include all members of a blended family.

_____

_____

_____

_____

_____

_____

7.4 Obituary/Eulogy

Education: _____

Employment: _____

Funeral/Memorial Service (include date, time, address, and city/town if obituary is in more than one publication):

_____

_____

Charitable Donations: _____

Photo Location: _____

Publication Name and City: _____

_____

Other: _____

_____

_____

_____

_____

_____

_____

_____

_____

_____

_____

_____

 ©2023 *Just in Case* by Elaine Lozinski. This material may not be altered, copied, or translated without permission of the author.

7.5 Funeral/Memorial: Notes

Notes

_____

_____

_____

_____

_____

_____

_____

_____

_____

_____

_____

_____

_____

_____

_____

_____

_____

_____

_____

_____

_____

_____

IMPORTANT
DOCUMENTATION

8.1 Important Documentation

Name: _____

Date Created
or Updated: _____

Document	Location
Birth Certificate	
Passport	
Social Insurance Number (SIN)	
Citizenship Card	
Naturalization Certificate	
Driver's Licence	
Marriage Licence	
Death Certificates	
Baptismal Certificate	
Divorce Agreement	
Separation Agreement	
Pre-nuptial Agreement	
Co-habitation Agreement	
Child Custody Agreement	
Child Support Agreement	
Immunization Records	
Diploma	
Report Cards	
Accreditation Documents	
Other	

©2023 *Just in Case* by Elaine Lozinski. This material may not be altered, copied, or translated without permission of the author.

FAMILY
INFORMATION

9.1-1 Family History: You

Name: _____

Date Created
or Updated: _____

Your Full Name: _____

Previous Names: _____

Father's Name: _____

Mother's Name: _____

Date of Birth: _____ Place of Birth: _____

Current Address: _____

_____

Spouse Name: _____

Previous Names: _____

Date of Birth: _____ Place of Birth: _____

Current Address: _____

_____

Date of Marriage: _____ Date of Death: _____

Children's Names: _____

_____

Notes: _____

_____

_____

_____

_____

9.1-1 Family History: You

Previous Spouse: _____

Previous Names: _____

Date of Birth: _____ Place of Birth: _____

Current Address: _____

_____

Date of Marriage: _____ Date of Divorce: _____

Date of Death: _____

Children's Names: _____

_____

Notes: _____

_____

_____

_____

_____

_____

_____

_____

_____

_____

 ©2023 *Just in Case* by Elaine Lozinski. This material may not be altered, copied, or translated without permission of the author.

9.1-2 Parents

Name: _____

Date Created or Updated: _____

Father Name: _____

Previous Names: _____

Date of Birth: _____ Place of Birth: _____

Current Address: _____

_____

Date of Death: _____

Mother Name: _____

Previous Names: _____

Date of Birth: _____ Place of Birth: _____

Current Address: _____

_____

Date of Death: _____

Date of Marriage: _____ Date of Divorce: _____

Children's Names: _____

Step-Parent Name: _____

Previous Names: _____

Date of Birth: _____ Place of Birth: _____

Current Address: _____

_____

Date of Death: _____

Date of Marriage: _____ Date of Divorce: _____

Children's Names: _____

©2023 *Just in Case* by Elaine Lozinski. This material may not be altered, copied, or translated without permission of the author.

Notes

_____

_____

_____

_____

_____

_____

_____

_____

_____

_____

_____

_____

_____

_____

_____

_____

_____

 ©2023 _Just in Case_ by Elaine Lozinski. This material may not be altered, copied, or translated without permission of the author.

9.1-3 Siblings

Name: _____

Date Created or Updated: _____

*Include all adopted and step-siblings.

Sibling Name: _____

Previous Names: _____

Father's Name: _____ Mother's Name: _____

Date of Birth: _____ Place of Birth: _____

Current Address: _____

_____

Date of Death: _____

Spouse Name: _____

Date of Marriage: _____

Children's Names: _____

_____

Sibling Name: _____

Previous Names: _____

Father's Name: _____ Mother's Name: _____

Date of Birth: _____ Place of Birth: _____

Current Address: _____

_____

Date of Death: _____

Spouse Name: _____

Date of Marriage: _____

Children's Names: _____

©2023 *Just in Case* by Elaine Lozinski. This material may not be altered, copied, or translated without permission of the author.

9.1-3 Siblings

Name: _____

Date Created or Updated: _____

***Include all adopted and step-siblings.**

Sibling Name: _____

Previous Names: _____

Father's Name: _____ Mother's Name: _____

Date of Birth: _____ Place of Birth: _____

Current Address: _____

_____

Date of Death: _____

Spouse Name: _____

Date of Marriage: _____

Children's Names: _____

_____

Sibling Name: _____

Previous Names: _____

Father's Name: _____ Mother's Name: _____

Date of Birth: _____ Place of Birth: _____

Current Address: _____

_____

Date of Death: _____

Spouse Name: _____

Date of Marriage: _____

Children's Names: _____

 ©2023 *Just in Case* by Elaine Lozinski. This material may not be altered, copied, or translated without permission of the author.

9.1-3 Siblings

Name: _____

Date Created or Updated: _____

*Include all adopted and step-siblings.

Sibling Name: _____

Previous Names: _____

Father's Name: _____ Mother's Name: _____

Date of Birth: _____ Place of Birth: _____

Current Address: _____

_____

Date of Death: _____

Spouse Name: _____

Date of Marriage: _____

Children's Names: _____

_____

Sibling Name: _____

Previous Names: _____

Father's Name: _____ Mother's Name: _____

Date of Birth: _____ Place of Birth: _____

Current Address: _____

_____

Date of Death: _____

Spouse Name: _____

Date of Marriage: _____

Children's Names: _____

©2023 *Just in Case* by Elaine Lozinski. This material may not be siltered, copied, or translated without permission of the author.

9.1-3 Siblings

Notes

_____

_____

_____

_____

_____

_____

_____

_____

_____

_____

_____

_____

_____

_____

_____

_____

©2023 *Just in Case* by Elaine Lozinski. This material may not be altered, copied, or translated without permission of the author.

9.1-4 Grandparents

Name: _____

Date Created or Updated: _____

Maternal Grandfather Name: _____

Previous Names: _____

Date of Birth: _____ Place of Birth: _____

Current Address: _____

_____

Date of Death: _____

Maternal Grandmother Name: _____

Previous Names: _____

Date of Birth: _____ Place of Birth: _____

Current Address: _____

_____

Date of Death: _____

Date of Marriage: _____ Date of Divorce: _____

Children's Names: _____

_____

Step-Grandparent Name: _____

Previous Names: _____

Date of Birth: _____ Place of Birth: _____

Current Address: _____

_____

Date of Death: _____

Date of Marriage: _____ Date of Divorce: _____

Children's Names: _____

©2023 *Just in Case* by Elaine Lozinski. This material may not be altered, copied, or translated without permission of the author.

9.1-4 Grandparents

Paternal Grandfather Name: _____

Previous Names: _____

Date of Birth: _____ Place of Birth: _____

Current Address: _____

_____

Date of Death: _____

Paternal Grandmother Name: _____

Previous Names: _____

Date of Birth: _____ Place of Birth: _____

Current Address: _____

_____

Date of Death: _____

Date of Marriage: _____ Date of Divorce: _____

Children's Names: _____

_____

Step-Grandparent Name: _____

Previous Names: _____

Date of Birth: _____ Place of Birth: _____

Current Address: _____

_____

Date of Death: _____

Date of Marriage: _____ Date of Divorce: _____

Children's Names: _____

_____

 ©2023 *Just in Case* by Elaine Lozinski. This material may not be altered, copied, or translated without permission of the author.

9.1-4 Grandparents

Notes

_____

_____

_____

_____

_____

_____

_____

_____

_____

_____

_____

_____

_____

_____

_____

_____

_____

©2023 *Just in Case* by Elaine Lozinski. This material may not be altered, copied, or translated without permission of the author.

9.1-5 Children

Name: _____

Date Created or Updated: _____

*Include all adopted and step children.

Child Name: _____

Previous Names: _____

Father's Name: _____ Mother's Name: _____

Date of Birth: _____ Place of Birth: _____

Current Address: _____

_____

Date of Death: _____

Spouse Name: _____

Date of Marriage: _____

Children's Names: _____

_____

Child Name: _____

Previous Names: _____

Father's Name: _____ Mother's Name: _____

Date of Birth: _____ Place of Birth: _____

Current Address: _____

_____

Date of Death: _____

Spouse Name: _____

Date of Marriage: _____

Children's Names: _____

©2023 *Just in Case* by Elaine Lozinski. This material may not be altered, copied, or translated without permission of the author.

9.1-5 Children

Child Name: _____

Previous Names: _____

Father's Name: _____ Mother's Name: _____

Date of Birth: _____ Place of Birth: _____

Current Address: _____

_____

Date of Death: _____

Spouse Name: _____

Date of Marriage: _____

Children's Names: _____

_____

Child Name: _____

Previous Names: _____

Father's Name: _____ Mother's Name: _____

Date of Birth: _____ Place of Birth: _____

Current Address: _____

_____

Date of Death: _____

Spouse Name: _____

Date of Marriage: _____

Children's Names: _____

_____

 ©2023 *Just in Case* by Elaine Lozinski. This material may not be altered, copied, or translated without permission of the author.

9.1-5 Children

Child Name: _____

Previous Names: _____

Father's Name: _____ Mother's Name: _____

Date of Birth: _____ Place of Birth: _____

Current Address: _____

_____

Date of Death: _____

Spouse Name: _____

Date of Marriage: _____

Children's Names: _____

_____

Child Name: _____

Previous Names: _____

Father's Name: _____ Mother's Name: _____

Date of Birth: _____ Place of Birth: _____

Current Address: _____

_____

Date of Death: _____

Spouse Name: _____

Date of Marriage: _____

Children's Names: _____

_____

©2023 *Just in Case* by Elaine Lozinski. This material may not be altered, copied, or translated without permission of the author.

9.1-5 Children

Notes

_____

_____

_____

_____

_____

_____

_____

_____

_____

_____

_____

_____

_____

_____

_____

_____

_____

©2023 *Just in Case* by Elaine Lozinski. This material may not be altered, copied, or translated without permission of the author.

9.1-6 Grandchildren

Name: _____

Date Created or Updated: _____

*Include all adopted and step-grandchildren.

Grandchild Name: _____

Previous Names: _____

Father's Name: _____ Mother's Name: _____

Date of Birth: _____ Place of Birth: _____

Current Address: _____

_____

Date of Death: _____

Spouse Name: _____

Date of Marriage: _____

Children's Names: _____

_____

Grandchild Name: _____

Previous Names: _____

Father's Name: _____ Mother's Name: _____

Date of Birth: _____ Place of Birth: _____

Current Address: _____

_____

Date of Death: _____

Spouse Name: _____

Date of Marriage: _____

Children's Names: _____

9.1-6 Grandchildren

Grandchild Name: _____

Previous Names: _____

Father's Name: _____ Mother's Name: _____

Date of Birth: _____ Place of Birth: _____

Current Address: _____

_____

Date of Death: _____

Spouse Name: _____

Date of Marriage: _____

Children's Names: _____

_____

Grandchild Name: _____

Previous Names: _____

Father's Name: _____ Mother's Name: _____

Date of Birth: _____ Place of Birth: _____

Current Address: _____

_____

Date of Death: _____

Spouse Name: _____

Date of Marriage: _____

Children's Names: _____

_____

 ©2023 *Just in Case* by Elaine Lozinski. This material may not be altered, copied, or translated without permission of the author.

9.1-6 Grandchildren

Grandchild Name: _____

Previous Names: _____

Father's Name: _____ Mother's Name: _____

Date of Birth: _____ Place of Birth: _____

Current Address: _____

_____

Date of Death: _____

Spouse Name: _____

Date of Marriage: _____

Children's Names: _____

_____

Grandchild Name: _____

Previous Names: _____

Father's Name: _____ Mother's Name: _____

Date of Birth: _____ Place of Birth: _____

Current Address: _____

_____

Date of Death: _____

Spouse Name: _____

Date of Marriage: _____

Children's Names: _____

_____

9.1-6 Grandchildren

Notes

_____

_____

_____

_____

_____

_____

_____

_____

_____

_____

_____

_____

_____

_____

_____

_____

 ©2023 *Just in Case* by Elaine Lozinski. This material may not be altered, copied, or translated without permission of the author.

9.1-7 Nieces & Nephews

Name: _____

Date Created or Updated: _____

*Include all adopted and step-children.

Name: _____

Previous Names: _____

Father's Name: _____ Mother's Name: _____

Date of Birth: _____ Place of Birth: _____

Current Address: _____

_____

Date of Death: _____

Spouse Name: _____

Date of Marriage: _____

Children's Names: _____

_____

Name: _____

Previous Names: _____

Father's Name: _____ Mother's Name: _____

Date of Birth: _____ Place of Birth: _____

Current Address: _____

_____

Date of Death: _____

Spouse Name: _____

Date of Marriage: _____

Children's Names: _____

©2023 *Just in Case* by Elaine Lozinski. This material may not be altered, copied, or translated without permission of the author.

9.1-7 Nieces & Nephews

Name: _____

Previous Names: _____

Father's Name: _____ Mother's Name: _____

Date of Birth: _____ Place of Birth: _____

Current Address: _____

_____

Date of Death: _____

Spouse Name: _____

Date of Marriage: _____

Children's Names: _____

_____

Name: _____

Previous Names: _____

Father's Name: _____ Mother's Name: _____

Date of Birth: _____ Place of Birth: _____

Current Address: _____

_____

Date of Death: _____

Spouse Name: _____

Date of Marriage: _____

Children's Names: _____

_____

Notes: _____

 ©2023 *Just in Case* by Elaine Lozinski. This material may not be altered, copied, or translated without permission of the author.

9.1-7 Nieces & Nephews

Name: _____

Previous Names: _____

Father's Name: _____ Mother's Name: _____

Date of Birth: _____ Place of Birth: _____

Current Address: _____

_____

Date of Death: _____

Spouse Name: _____

Date of Marriage: _____

Children's Names: _____

_____

Name: _____

Previous Names: _____

Father's Name: _____ Mother's Name: _____

Date of Birth: _____ Place of Birth: _____

Current Address: _____

_____

Date of Death: _____

Spouse Name: _____

Date of Marriage: _____

Children's Names: _____

_____

Notes: _____

©2023 *Just in Case* by Elaine Lozinski. This material may not be altered, copied, or translated without permission of the author.

9.1-7 Nieces & Nephews

Notes

_____

_____

_____

_____

_____

_____

_____

_____

_____

_____

_____

_____

_____

_____

_____

_____

 ©2023 *Just in Case* by Elaine Lozinski. This material may not be altered, copied, or translated without permission of the author.

9.1-8 Uncles & Aunts

Name: _____

Date Created or Updated: _____

Maternal Uncle or Aunt: _____

Previous Names: _____

Date of Birth: _____ Date of Death: _____

Spouse Name _____

Current Address: _____

_____

Children: _____

_____

Maternal Uncle or Aunt: _____

Previous Names: _____

Date of Birth: _____ Date of Death: _____

Spouse Name _____

Current Address: _____

_____

Children: _____

_____

Maternal Uncle or Aunt: _____

Previous Names: _____

Date of Birth: _____ Date of Death: _____

Spouse Name _____

Current Address: _____

_____

Children: _____

9.1-8 Uncles & Aunts

Name: _____

Date Created or Updated: _____

Maternal Uncle or Aunt: _____

Previous Names: _____

Date of Birth: _____ Date of Death: _____

Spouse Name _____

Current Address: _____

_____

Children: _____

_____

Maternal Uncle or Aunt: _____

Previous Names: _____

Date of Birth: _____ Date of Death: _____

Spouse Name _____

Current Address: _____

_____

Children: _____

_____

Maternal Uncle or Aunt: _____

Previous Names: _____

Date of Birth: _____ Date of Death: _____

Spouse Name _____

Current Address: _____

_____

Children: _____

 ©2023 *Just in Case* by Elaine Lozinski. This material may not be altered, copied, or translated without permission of the author.

9.1-8 Uncles & Aunts

Paternal Uncle or Aunt: _____

Previous Names: _____

Date of Birth: _____ Date of Death: _____

Spouse Name _____

Current Address: _____

_____

Children: _____

_____

Paternal Uncle or Aunt: _____

Previous Names: _____

Date of Birth: _____ Date of Death: _____

Spouse Name _____

Current Address: _____

_____

Children: _____

_____

Paternal Uncle or Aunt: _____

Previous Names: _____

Date of Birth: _____ Date of Death: _____

Spouse Name _____

Current Address: _____

_____

Children: _____

_____

9.1-8 Uncles & Aunts

Paternal Uncle or Aunt: _____

Previous Names: _____

Date of Birth: _____ Date of Death: _____

Spouse Name _____

Current Address: _____

_____

Children: _____

_____

Paternal Uncle or Aunt: _____

Previous Names: _____

Date of Birth: _____ Date of Death: _____

Spouse Name _____

Current Address: _____

_____

Children: _____

_____

Paternal Uncle or Aunt: _____

Previous Names: _____

Date of Birth: _____ Date of Death: _____

Spouse Name _____

Current Address: _____

_____

Children: _____

_____

 ©2023 *Just in Case* by Elaine Lozinski. This material may not be altered, copied, or translated without permission of the author.

9.1-8 Uncles & Aunts

Notes

_____

_____

_____

_____

_____

_____

_____

_____

_____

_____

_____

_____

_____

_____

_____

_____

_____

©2023 *Just in Case* by Elaine Lozinski. This material may not be altered, copied, or translated without permission of the author.

9.1-9 Family: Other

Name: _____

Date Created
or Updated: _____

Include other family members or close family friends you feel are important.

_____

_____

_____

_____

_____

_____

_____

_____

_____

_____

_____

_____

_____

_____

_____

9.2-1 Important Dates

Name: _____

Date Created
or Updated: _____

Include important dates, such as weddings, divorces, deaths, baptisms, graduations, etc.

Event: _____

Date: _____

Notes: _____

_____

Event: _____

Date: _____

Notes: _____

_____

Event: _____

Date: _____

Notes: _____

_____

Event: _____

Date: _____

Notes: _____

_____

Event: _____

Date: _____

Notes: _____

©2023 *Just in Case* by Elaine Lozinski. This material may not be altered, copied, or translated without permission of the author.

9.2-1 Important Dates

Notes

_____

_____

_____

_____

_____

_____

_____

_____

_____

_____

_____

_____

_____

_____

_____

_____

 ©2023 *Just in Case* by Elaine Lozinski. This material may not be altered, copied, or translated without permission of the author.

9.2-2 Address History

Name: _____

Date Created or Updated: _____

Include all places of residence.

Address: _____

_____

Year(s): _____

Notes: _____

_____

Address: _____

_____

Year(s): _____

Notes: _____

_____

Address: _____

_____

Year(s): _____

Notes: _____

_____

Address: _____

_____

Year(s): _____

Notes: _____

_____

©2023 *Just in Case* by Elaine Lozinski. This material may not be altered, copied, or translated without permission of the author.

9.2-2 Address History

Address: _____

_____

Year(s): _____

Notes: _____

_____

Address: _____

_____

Year(s): _____

Notes: _____

_____

Address: _____

_____

Year(s): _____

Notes: _____

_____

Address: _____

_____

Year(s): _____

Notes: _____

_____

_____

_____

©2023 *Just in Case* by Elaine Lozinski. This material may not be altered, copied, or translated without permission of the author.

9.2-3 Family Memories/Stories

Name: _____

Date Created or Updated: _____

Include any memoirs or any family stories you wish to record.

_____

_____

_____

_____

_____

_____

_____

_____

_____

_____

_____

_____

_____

_____

_____

_____

_____

9.2-3 Family Memories/Stories

 ©2023 *Just in Case* by Elaine Lozinski. This material may not be altered, copied, or translated without permission of the author.

9.2-4 Family Data: Other

Name: _____

Date Created or Updated: _____

Include any family data you feel is important.

_____

_____

_____

_____

_____

_____

_____

_____

_____

_____

_____

_____

_____

_____

_____

_____

_____

_____

_____

©2023 *Just in Case* by Elaine Lozinski. This material may not be altered, copied, or translated without permission of the author.

9.2-4 Family Data: Other

_____

_____

_____

_____

_____

_____

_____

_____

_____

_____

_____

_____

_____

_____

_____

_____

_____

_____

_____

©2023 *Just in Case* by Elaine Lozinski. This material may not be altered, copied, or translated without permission of the author.

9.3-1 Letters to Loved Ones

Name: _____

Date Created or Updated: _____

Write letters to loved ones for times and events when you can't be there.

_____

_____

_____

_____

_____

_____

_____

_____

_____

_____

_____

_____

_____

_____

_____

_____

_____

©2023 *Just in Case* by Elaine Lozinski. This material may not be altered, copied, or translated without permission of the author.

9.3-1 Letters to Loved Ones

_____

_____

_____

_____

_____

_____

_____

_____

_____

_____

_____

_____

_____

_____

_____

_____

_____

 ©2023 *Just in Case* by Elaine Lozinski. This material may not be altered, copied, or translated without permission of the author.

9.3-2 Memorabilia

Name: _____

Date Created or Updated: _____

Include any memorabilia you feel is important. Include favorite/traditional family recipes, newspaper clippings, birth or death announcements, school report cards, military decorations, etc.

_____
_____
_____
_____
_____
_____
_____
_____
_____
_____
_____
_____
_____
_____
_____
_____
_____

9.3-2 Memorabilia

_____

_____

_____

_____

_____

_____

_____

_____

_____

_____

_____

_____

_____

_____

_____

_____

_____

_____

_____

©2023 *Just in Case* by Elaine Lozinski. This material may not be altered, copied, or translated without permission of the author.

9.3-3 Family: Other Information

Name: _____

Date Created or Updated: _____

Include any other important history or family information.

_____

_____

_____

_____

_____

_____

_____

_____

_____

_____

_____

_____

_____

_____

_____

_____

9.3-3 Family: Other Information

_____

_____

_____

_____

_____

_____

_____

_____

_____

_____

_____

_____

_____

_____

_____

_____

_____

©2023 *Just in Case* by Elaine Lozinski. This material may not be altered, copied, or translated without permission of the author.

PHILANTHROPY
AND CHARITY

10.1 Philanthropy/Charity

Name: _____

Date Created or Updated: _____

Charity Name: _____

Telephone: _____

Contact Name: _____

Address: _____

_____

Donation History: _____

_____

Intention: _____

_____

Notes: _____

Charity Name: _____

Telephone: _____

Contact Name: _____

Address: _____

_____

Donation History: _____

_____

Intention: _____

_____

Notes: _____

©2023 *Just in Case* by Elaine Lozinski. This material may not be altered, copied, or translated without permission of the author.

OTHER CONSIDERATIONS

11.1 Pets

Name: _____

Date Created or Updated: _____

Are Pets Mentioned in the Will? _____

Pet Name: _____

Breed: _____

Date of Birth: _____

Pet Licence Number: _____ Registration Chip Number: _____

Veterinarian Clinic: _____

Address: _____

Pet Name: _____

Breed: _____

Date of Birth: _____

Pet Licence Number: _____ Registration Chip Number: _____

Temporary Guardian (In Case of Emergency)

Name: _____

Phone: _____

Email: _____

Address: _____

Permanent Guardian

Name: _____

Phone: _____

Email: _____

Address: _____

©2023 *Just in Case* by Elaine Lozinski. This material may not be altered, copied, or translated without permission of the author.

11.1 Pets

Feeding or other care instructions: _____

_____

_____

_____

_____

_____

_____

_____

_____

Notes: _____

_____

_____

_____

_____

_____

_____

_____

_____

 ©2023 *Just in Case* by Elaine Lozinski. This material may not be altered, copied, or translated without permission of the author.

11.2 Housing

Name: _____

Date Created
or Updated: _____

Aging in Place

Renovations/upgrades that may be required: _____

_____

_____

_____

_____

_____

_____

At home Care Providers: _____

_____

_____

_____

_____

_____

_____

Notes: _____

_____

_____

_____

_____

_____

11.2 Housing

Downsizing/Senior Living

Condos, rentals, Retirement Communities, etc. you are considering: _____

Life Lease or Rent?: _____

Cost per month: _____

Meals provided: _____

Amenities: _____

Activities offered: _____

Level of Care Available: _____

Unit Description: _____

_____

Wait List: _____

_____

Notes: _____

_____

_____

_____

_____

_____

_____

_____

_____

_____

©2023 *Just in Case* by Elaine Lozinski. This material may not be altered, copied, or translated without permission of the author.

11.3 Retirement Plan

Name: _____

Date Created or Updated: _____

Projected Retirement Date
or Date Retired: _____

Retirement Plan

Where applicable, describe your work/retirement transition plan.

_____

_____

_____

_____

_____

_____

_____

Financial Retirement Plan

Outline current financial retirement plan. For further information see the Financial Information chapter of *Just in Case*. Reassess every six months to ensure you keep on track with the plan. Review annually with your financial planner.

_____

_____

_____

_____

_____

_____

_____

_____

©2023 *Just in Case* by Elaine Lozinski. This material may not be altered, copied, or translated without permission of the author.

11.3 Retirement Plan

Travel

List your travel destination bucket list. Consider places around your city, region, country or the world. Estimate time frames and research costs.

_____

_____

_____

_____

_____

_____

_____

_____

To-Do Lists

List or identify tasks in your life or around your home that you can now undertake.

_____

_____

_____

_____

_____

_____

_____

_____

_____

_____

_____

 ©2023 *Just in Case* by Elaine Lozinski. This material may not be altered, copied, or translated without permission of the author.

11.3 Retirement Plan

Fitness/Activity

List daily or weekly activities and past times, such as volunteer work, part-time work, social clubs, etc. that engage you mentally and socially.

_____

_____

_____

_____

_____

_____

_____

_____

List or identify activities or pastimes you enjoy to maintain year-round fitness.

_____

_____

_____

_____

_____

_____

_____

_____

_____

_____

_____

_____

©2023 *Just in Case* by Elaine Lozinski. This material may not be altered, copied, or translated without permission of the author.

11.3 Retirement Plan

Health/Nutrition

List any health appointments, health issues or concerns you may have. Think about a timeline to take care of these matters.

_____

_____

_____

_____

_____

_____

_____

_____

Review your weekly diet and vitamin and supplement intake. Write down any areas that can be improved and identify ways to implement change. Consider consulting a nutritionist.

_____

_____

_____

_____

_____

_____

_____

_____

_____

_____

 ©2023 *Just in Case* by Elaine Lozinski. This material may not be altered, copied, or translated without permission of the author.

11.4 De-Clutter

Name: _____

Date Created
or Updated: _____

List people, organizations, charities, etc. that will help, take or receive donations for your downsized possessions.

_____

_____

_____

_____

_____

_____

_____

_____

_____

_____

Notes: _____

_____

_____

_____

_____

11.5 Shared Knowledge

Name: _____

Date Created
or Updated: _____

Identify roles or situations where a partner may require more knowledge or guidance. Provide names of people or organizations that may assist and write out instructions.

_____

_____

_____

_____

_____

_____

_____

_____

_____

_____

_____

Notes: _____

_____

_____

_____

_____

©2023 *Just in Case* by Elaine Lozinski. This material may not be altered, copied, or translated without permission of the author.

11.6 Final Thoughts

Name: _____

Date Created
or Updated: _____

List or identify any other areas of Final Affair planning not covered in *Just in Case*.

_____

_____

_____

_____

_____

_____

_____

_____

_____

_____

_____

Notes: _____

_____

_____

_____

_____

©2023 *Just in Case* by Elaine Lozinski. This material may not be altered, copied, or translated without permission of the author.

About the Author

ELAINE LOZINSKI is a Final Affair consultant, author and Certified Executor Advisor with the Canadian Institute of Certified Executor Advisors, who strives to bring clarity to the overwhelming world of final affairs. Along with individual consulting, Elaine gives lectures across western Canada delivering a popular seminar on final affairs.

A planner by nature, Elaine wanted to leverage her love of organization along with her desire to teach and help people be prepared for emergency, incapacity, end of life, and other support situations... just in case. Elaine's goal with *Just in Case: Final Affair Arrangements* is to educate, prepare, and empower people to make their own decisions regarding their final affairs - before something happens.

Elaine lives in Saskatoon, Saskatchewan, Canada, and when she is not busy working, she can usually be found at her cabin with her husband, dog, and at least one of her six grown children.

To learn more about Elaine and her work visit www.justincasebinder.ca.

Acknowledgments

I am very grateful for all of those who have given me their support and encouragement of this book by sharing with me their personal experiences and family stories.

I would like to acknowledge Harold Empey for the original concept of this book. I am enormously grateful for having had his friendship and partnership. I am honored that he entrusted me to continue what he started.

I would like to thank those who have provided information and assistance in the process of writing this book. Your help made it all possible. I would specifically like to thank Elke Churchman, BA, LLB, for her guidance with the legal aspects of this book, my editor, Fay Thompson, and Lindsay Earle, who helped shape and polish this book.

Above all, I would like to thank my husband, Darren. I am forever grateful for your love, understanding and patience with me as I forge on with my passion. I am very blessed to be married to you.

REQUEST A *JUST IN CASE: FINAL AFFAIR ARRANGEMENTS* SEMINAR

The *Just in Case: Final Affair Arrangements* seminars and speaking engagements create an open and honest discussion about what it means to plan your final affairs. They bring clarity to the many common questions around final affair planning and discusses the practical ways to approach this work.

These presentations are for those interested in the following areas:

Final Affair Education

Estate Planning

Retirement Planning

Succession Planning

Family Assistance

Preparation for Power of Attorney and Executor Roles

These seminars are suitable for the following groups or organizations:

Financial Institutions and Professionals

Legal and Accounting Firms

Real Estate and Insurance Professionals

Health and Mental Health Organizations

Funeral Service Providers

Social, Senior and Community Groups

Employers and Employee Assistance Programs

Charity and Philanthropic Organizations

Family Offices

Clients

For further information, speaking fees and availability, please visit:
www.justincasebinder.ca

www.ingramcontent.com/pod-product-compliance
Lightning Source LLC
Chambersburg PA
CBHW081001140626
46546CB00018B/2860